T0116464

THE PSYCHOLOGY OF MEMORY

How can I improve my memory? Do my emotions affect my memories? How will my memory change as I get older?

The Psychology of Memory provides a unique insight into a fundamental part of being human, debunking many common misconceptions about what memory is, how memory works, and the accuracy of our memories. It explores the complexity of human memory, looking at how we remember different types of information and the impact of issues like aging and emotion on how we create, store, and retrieve memories. Extremes of memory from so-called photographic memory to dementia are discussed, along with ways our memory can impact our everyday lives in educational and legal settings.

Treating memory as malleable, dynamic, and active, *The Psychology of Memory* teaches us about how our individual memories function, and how we can harness this to see memory in a new way; to use the past, our experiences and information, in service of the present and future.

Megan Sumeracki is an associate professor of psychology at Rhode Island College, USA. She is a cognitive psychologist and memory expert, and is well-known for her work on evidence-based practice in education.

Althea Need Kaminske is the senior director of Student Academic Support and Achievement at Indiana University School of Medicine, USA. She is a cognitive psychologist and memory expert, and is well-regarded for her work on evidence-based practice in education.

THE PSYCHOLOGY OF EVERYTHING

People are fascinated by psychology, and what makes humans tick. Why do we think and behave the way we do? We've all met armchair psychologists claiming to have the answers, and people that ask if psychologists can tell what they're thinking. The Psychology of Everything is a series of books which debunk the popular myths and pseudo-science surrounding some of life's biggest questions.

The series explores the hidden psychological factors that drive us, from our subconscious desires and aversions, to our natural social instincts. Absorbing, informative, and always intriguing, each book is written by an expert in the field, examining how research-based knowledge compares with popular wisdom, and showing how psychology can truly enrich our understanding of modern life.

Applying a psychological lens to an array of topics and contemporary concerns—from sex, to fashion, to conspiracy theories—The Psychology of Everything will make you look at everything in a new way.

Titles in the series:

For more information about this series, please visit: www.routledge textbooks.com/textbooks/thepsychologyofeverything/

THE PSYCHOLOGY OF MEMORY

MEGAN SUMERACKI AND ALTHEA NEED KAMINSKE

Routledge
Taylor & Francis Group

LONDON AND NEW YORK

Designed cover image

First published 2024
by Routledge
4 Park Square, Milton Park, Abingdon, Oxon OX14 4RN

and by Routledge
605 Third Avenue, New York, NY 10158

Routledge is an imprint of the Taylor & Francis Group, an informa business

British Library Cataloguing-in-Publication Data
A catalogue record for this book is available from the British Library

Library of Congress Cataloging-in-Publication Data
Names: Sumeracki, Megan, author. | Kaminske, Althea Need, author.
Title: The psychology of memory / Megan Sumeracki and Althea
    Need Kaminske.
Description: First Edition. | New York, NY : Routledge, 2024. |
    Series: The psychology of everything | Includes bibliographical
    references.
Identifiers: LCCN 2023052454 (print) | LCCN 2023052455
    (ebook) | ISBN 9781032488639 (paperback) | ISBN
    9781032488646 (hardback) | ISBN 9781003391166 (ebook)
Subjects: LCSH: Memory. | Cognitive psychology.
Classification: LCC BF371 .S946 2024 (print) | LCC BF371
    (ebook) | DDC 153.1/2—dc23/eng/20231113
LC record available at https://lccn.loc.gov/2023052454
LC ebook record available at https://lccn.loc.gov/2023052455

ISBN: 978-1-032-48864-6 (hbk)
ISBN: 978-1-032-48863-9 (pbk)
ISBN: 978-1-003-39116-6 (ebk)

DOI: 10.4324/9781003391166

Typeset in Joanna
by Apex CoVantage, LLC

CONTENTS

ABOUT THE AUTHORS

Megan Sumeracki earned her MA in experimental psychology at Washington University in St. Louis, and her PhD in cognitive psychology at Purdue University. She is now an associate professor of psychology at Rhode Island College. She is one of the original co-founders of The Learning Scientists, a co-author of the award-winning book *Understanding How We Learn: A Visual Guide*, and the lead author of *Ace That Test: A Student's Guide to Learning Better*. In her free time, Megan enjoys crocheting, scrapbooking and general crafting, and traveling to new places to hike and go wine tasting. She lives in Rhode Island in the US with her husband, Sam, daughter, Molly, and cat, Teddy.

Althea Need Kaminske earned her PhD in cognitive psychology at Purdue University and is now an associate clinical professor of surgery and the senior director of Student Academic Support and Achievement at Indiana University School of Medicine. She is a co-author of the books *Five Teaching and Learning Myths—Debunked* and *Ace That Test: A Student's Guide to Learning Better*. In her free time, Althea enjoys going on walks with her family, reading science fiction, fantasy, and romance, and playing *Dungeons & Dragons*. She lives in Indianapolis, Indiana, in the US with her husband, Tim, son, Calvin, dog, Bree, and cat, Sushi.

Both Megan and Althea are members of the Learning Scientists Team (www.learningscientists.org). They frequently give talks and workshops around the world about the effective and efficient use of the science of learning and memory in the classroom and other learning settings such as museums, the US State Department, hospitals, corporate settings, and more. You can follow the Learning Scientists on X/Twitter: @AceThatTest.

ACKNOWLEDGMENTS

We first extend our immense gratitude to our fellow Learning Scientists team members, Carolina Kuepper-Tetzel and Cynthia Nebel. Without them, we are confident we would not have been able to write this book. We also thank the many teachers, students, parents, and other educators who engage with the Learning Scientists community; you really help keep us motivated in our work.

We thank our advisors: Jeffrey Karpicke, David Pisoni, and Henry "Roddy" Roediger, who taught us about memory and academia, and about writing and collaborating with others. We also want to thank our students and colleagues at Rhode Island College, Indiana University School of Medicine, and St. Bonaventure University, and the many institutions at which we have learned, worked, and taught in the past.

Megan would like to thank: My husband, Sam, for his love, support, and encouragement while writing this book and throughout my career as a whole. I would also like to acknowledge my children: Spencer, who left this world far too soon but will never be forgotten, and Molly, the rainbow light of my life. Thank you to my mom, Sandy, who is always supportive whether near or far, and gave me a rich example that illustrates how problematic very early childhood memories can be! (No one blames you for the burn, Mom. You are the best.) Finally, thanks to little Ellie cat who was with me from the beginning of graduate school in St. Louis all the way through becoming an associate professor in Rhode Island (and lived in two more states in between). I even miss when Ellie would march on the keyboard, even though that slows my writing down.

Althea would like to thank: My family for their support, encouragement, and understanding during the writing process. I would also like to thank my friends and colleagues for being a supportive audience for my many stories and "memory fun facts" collected during the writing of this book.

Finally, we would like to thank our editors Ceri McLardy, Emilie Coin, and other helpful staff at Routledge, and Andrea Dottolo and Cynthia Nebel for their helpful advice, comments, and word-reduction suggestions.

1

INTRODUCTION

When we tell people that we study memory, often their first response is to tell us how bad their memory is. They are worried that either their memory is getting worse or that it was never good to begin with. They are ready with examples of times they forgot their keys, the name of an acquaintance, or an important anniversary. If only, they lament, they had better memories, they would not forget anything. However, memory researchers know that forgetting is a crucial part of memory. For example, Jill Price was diagnosed with highly superior autobiographical memory (HSAM), a condition that leads her to have highly vivid and detailed memories of her life. Rather than being overjoyed at her heightened memory ability, Price describes her memory as *uncontrollable, tyrannical*, and exhausting.[1] While most people would like to remember more, Price would like to remember less (see Chapter 4).

Memory, as we will argue throughout this book, is more complex, spans more areas, and involves more nuance than people often think. It touches every aspect of our lives. It is somewhat challenging, then, to give a brief yet accurate description of all the nuanced ways memory affects us. But we will try. In this first chapter, we provide an introduction to the topic of memory, and a brief history of cognitive psychology, the lens through which we understand memory. In Chapter 2, we discuss memory types and systems. Memory, contrary to how people might typically think about it, is not a single process. In

DOI: 10.4324/9781003391166-1

Chapter 3, we describe how memory works throughout the lifespan. Our memory systems function differently as we age, with peaks and declines occurring at different timepoints. In Chapter 4, we discuss the extremes of memory. Extremes of memory ability—from superior memory to amnesia—are somewhat rare and are often misrepresented in TV and film. In Chapter 5, we discuss memory and emotion. Emotion, stressors, and trauma can all affect our memory in complicated ways. In Chapter 6, we cover memory and education. Here our focus is on how the science of memory can be used to improve educational outcomes. In Chapter 7, we discuss memory and expertise. This chapter outlines how experts can enhance their capacity to remember information in their area of expertise, and how they think and remember differently from nonexperts. Finally, in Chapter 8, we cover memory and the law. Our ability to remember, and our confidence in our memories, has important ramifications for the legal system.

Indeed, memory seems to be a pervasive presence in almost every aspect of life. As cognitive psychologists, memory researchers, and professors, we are excited to share the research on memory with you. But we also have a specific point of view based on our background and training as cognitive psychologists. In this chapter we define memory and provide some of the history of cognitive psychology to provide some context.

WHAT IS MEMORY?

Because we are most aware of our memory when we have trouble remembering something, our intuitions about how memory works might be a little biased. For example, I (Althea) spend an embarrassing amount of time looking for my phone, water bottle, and keys. Leaving the house is a bit of a production, especially when I need to coordinate my efforts with my toddler. I usually have several false starts where I realize that someone's water bottle or emotional support item (for my toddler, it is a toy or random kitchen item; for me, it is my phone) has been left on the counter and I have to go back in to get it. Ironically, this seems to get harder, not easier, when I am leaving the house with my partner. There is an extra layer of communication that has to happen; and, if we are not on top of our game, we erroneously assume that the other grabbed the water bottle/snack/emotional support tongs. As a researcher I know this is because parenting a small child requires a lot of attention switching and disrupted sleep schedules, but as a person trying to get to work in the morning, it certainly feels like my memory could be better.

You may be unsurprised to learn that our memory systems are not necessarily designed to remember where we put our phones. Or keys. Or water bottles. Though we would hazard a guess that if we were in a survival scenario where dehydration was a concern, we would be much more aware of water sources. In fact, people are better at remembering information when they process it in a fitness-relevant scenario, such as being stranded in the grasslands of a foreign land.[2] And, while this book is about human memory, it is also interesting to note that some birds (crows, jays, magpies, etc.) have incredible memory for where food is stored. Not only can they remember the locations of hundreds of food caches, they return to the food based on perishability, ensuring that they eat the food before it goes bad.[3] On the other hand, I (Althea) can barely stay on top of the bananas that are on the counter in plain view and am regularly disappointed in my memory for what leftovers are in the fridge. Maybe if I was a bird, my memory would be better at this. It may be tempting to think that human memory is superior to that of animals, but if we think of memory as the ability to use the past in service of the present, we see a range of abilities across species that depend on the specific needs of the animals.

The purpose, and the definition of memory we use in this book, is *the use of the past, our experiences and information, in service of the present and future.* Our memories are not static records stored in a filing cabinet. Our memories are malleable, dynamic, and active. The purpose of memory is not to catalog your life as an unbiased observer. Our definition of memory is a functional one that we find really useful. In this view of memory, we look at supposed failures of memory and ask whether they can tell us something about how memory functions, rather than being disappointed that it does not work the way we think it should.

HOW DO SCIENTISTS STUDY MEMORY? A BRIEF HISTORY OF COGNITIVE SCIENCE

There are a lot of interesting twists and turns in the story of the early schools of thought in psychology. We will relay some of them here to demonstrate that scientists are people who, just like anyone else, have complicated relationships, motives, and histories; the development of any field relies on active debate and criticism; and our understanding of memory is shaped by the history of the methods, and therefore the people, of cognitive psychology.

EARLY PSYCHOLOGY AND MEMORY RESEARCH: WUNDT, JAMES, AND EBBINGHAUS

Experimental psychology emerged from the related fields of physiology and philosophy. Today, it may seem a little strange to say that physiology and philosophy are related. Physiology falls firmly within the sciences, while philosophy is within the humanities. However, this is a somewhat recent division. Historically, philosophy has been the domain of any rigorous reasoning and explanations about the nature of the universe. Many of the fields that are considered part of the natural sciences developed from fields of natural philosophy. Today, we use science to describe any field that uses the scientific method. However, while the scientific method was developed in the seventeenth century, it did not come into popular use until the twentieth century, with the publication of American educational philosopher John Dewey's book, *How We Think*, in 1910.[4] Therefore, in the late nineteenth century, philosophy and physiology were not perceived as being vastly different endeavors. And so, the history of experimental psychology, and, by extension, cognitive psychology and the scientific study of memory, starts with Wilhelm Maximilian Wundt, a German physiologist and philosopher who is credited with founding the first experimental psychology laboratory in 1879.

Wundt was interested in the relationship between physical sensations (i.e., sight, sound, etc.) and our conscious and unconscious interpretations of those sensations. However, Wundt had many domains of interest and set out to define psychology as a science, advocating for the use of experimental methods that were found in the natural sciences. He was influential not just for the breadth and depth of his research but for his mentorship. Throughout his career he trained 185 doctoral students, nearly half of whom were foreigners, many of whom went on to become prominent psychologists and philosophers in their home countries.[5] Thus, many of the early experimental psychologists were either directly or indirectly influenced by Wundt.

Similar to Wundt, William James was an instructor of physiology, philosophy, and psychology at Harvard from 1873–1907. James is also credited as co-founding pragmatism in philosophy and coining the phrase "stream of consciousness". In 1874 James taught the first course in psychology offered at Harvard University. James was a prolific writer in both psychology and philosophy. He published over 300 works—books, articles, reviews, essays, etc.[6] In psychology his most influential work is *The Principles of Psychology*,[7] which is remarkable in its descriptions of various psychological phenomena and is eminently quotable even now, some 130 years later. Here, James defined memory as "the knowledge of a former state of mind after it has already once dropped from consciousness".[7(p. 648)] He goes on to further describe what today we would call episodic memory (see Chapter 2).

> Memory requires more than mere dating of a fact in the past. It must be dated in MY past. . . . A general feeling of the past direction in time, then, a particular date conceived as a lying along a direction, and defined by its name or phenomenal contents, as an event imagined as located tethering, and owned as

part of my experience,—such are the elements of every act of memory.[7](p. 650)

Unlike Wundt, James was famed for his writing and teaching as opposed to his research. In fact, he had little interest in research and recruited the German psychologist Hugo Münsterberg to establish the first psychology laboratory at Harvard. James was interested in addressing wide audiences, and, in addition to his lectures at Harvard, he developed a series of lectures for teachers, famously stating that "psychology is a science and teaching is an art".[8]

Hermann Ebbinghaus is credited with conducting the first systematic experimental investigations in human memory. Ebbinghaus received his PhD in 1873 and eventually taught at the University of Berlin, but was not a member of a department of psychology or a research laboratory. He was just a rigorous and meticulous researcher who loved memory. His monograph *Über das Gedächtnis* (*Concerning Memory*) was published in 1885.[9]

Using himself as his own research subject, Ebbinghaus measured the relationship between repetition, subsequent relearning, and time. Many of the foundational principles of memory are described in this set of experiments. In one experiment, he learned 8 lists of 13 nonsense syllables until he could perfectly recall them twice in a row. Nonsense syllables were created by forming consonant-vowel-consonant syllables (e.g., *tid*, *buk*, etc.) and are still used in memory research today. After different intervals of time, he attempted to relearn the list of nonsense syllables and recorded how long it took to recall them twice in a row again. Based on this, he calculated a savings in relearning score. The smaller the number of repetitions, the greater the savings! This can also be converted into a measure of forgetting. His work showed that forgetting happens at a very fast rate initially, but then slows (see Figure 1.1). More than half of the information is forgotten within the first hour, but the amount of information forgotten after a day is not much different than after a week or a month. This forgetting curve is still widely used to explain forgetting and memory today.

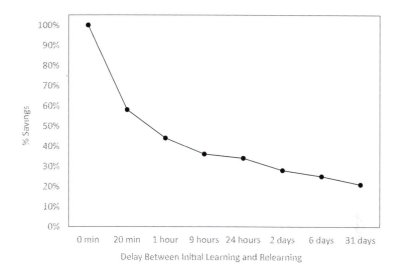

Figure 1.1 This figure shows the forgetting curve based on data from Ebbinghaus in 1885.[9] The figure shows the percent savings in relearning as a function of delay between initial learning and relearning. The most substantial drop in savings, or the rate of forgetting, happens within the first 20 minutes. While savings continue to decrease over time, it slows substantially so that there is not much difference in memory from 6 to 31 days.

Ebbinghaus did not publish further in memory. He did some research in physiological psychology and intelligence but, unlike Wundt, did not have a large following of his own. While his work was massively influential, and continues to be cited some 140 years later, with no students to carry on his work, his rigorous approach to memory research was somewhat isolated. From our viewpoint in the twenty-first century, both Ebbinghaus and James had remarkably modern methods and understandings of memory. Why were these ideas not systematically studied and developed in the upcoming twentieth century? Here we have one of the first twists in the history of the science of memory, and it can be traced back to one of Wundt's most famous students: Titchener.

WUNDT'S STUDENTS: TITCHENER AND MÜNSTERBERG

By 1892 Wundt's ideas had crossed the Atlantic to Cornell University in America in the form of Edward Bradford Titchener, an English psychologist and student of Wundt's. Titchener believed that psychology should be studied like the natural sciences, specifically chemistry. Whereas chemistry broke chemicals down into their component parts—elements like hydrogen and oxygen—psychology should break the mind down into its component parts, its mental elements. This school of thought is known as structuralism because it attempts to discover the structure of the mind. To Titchener, structuralism was the only way to study psychology, and anyone who did not follow structuralism was not a psychologist.[5] Titchener's legacy and importance in the field of psychology was immortalized by his student Edwin Garrigues Boring. Boring was a fervent admirer of Titchener, and he wrote *A History of Experimental Psychology*,[10] which was very influential in the twentieth century (and even still over 60 years later when we were in graduate school).

One of the main tools that Titchener used to study these elements was systematic introspection. He had very precise guidelines on his method of introspection, but the main idea was to ask people to describe a stimulus (like a piece of paper) by describing its characteristics (color, length, shape, etc.). Importantly, they could not just say the name of the thing ("paper") because the goal was to break it down into its component parts.

Another of Wundt's students, Hugo Münsterberg, also came to the United States to found a highly influential laboratory. Münsterberg was a prolific writer and, in stark contrast to Titchener, argued that psychology should be both practical and relevant. He was interested in the application of psychology to the fields of education, medicine, criminology, business, industry, and advertising. He compared the study of psychology to understanding water—that it was more natural to drink it than to analyze its chemical elements.[5] He is often considered to be the first industrial psychologist, contributed to forensic psychology, and had a long interest in mental illness. He wrote 32 books and 61 major papers throughout his career. Despite serving as chair of the psychology department at Harvard, president of the American Psychological Association, member of the Nobel Prize nominating committee for physiology or medicine, Münsterberg's contributions to psychology are often overlooked. Münsterberg, who was born in Prussia, tried to combat negative stereotypes of Germans in the years leading up to WWI, which led to public and professional backlash. Thus, while Münsterberg's approach to psychology is much closer to modern approaches, it was Tichener's work in structuralism that is discussed in textbooks today.

FUNCTIONALISM AND GESTALT

As experimental psychologists were exploring questions about the mind and behavior, several different schools of thought were developed. In James and Münsterberg, we can see the beginnings of functionalism. Functionalism emphasizes investigating the purpose of behavior, and is heavily influenced by Darwinian ideas around fitness and survival. Functionalists dismissed structuralism, likening trying to understand the mind by looking at its parts to trying to understand a house by analyzing its bricks and mortar.[11]

There were several notable proponents of functionalism: John Dewey (noted earlier for popularizing the term scientific method), James Angell, Edward Thorndike, and Mary Whiton Calkins, to name a few prominent psychologists of the time. Calkins is of particular interest for students of memory because she pioneered the use of paired-associate learning, a methodology that is heavily used in memory research today. Her method involved showing a series of colors paired with numbers, then testing the memory of the numbers when shown the colors. She demonstrated that while numbers were remembered better when paired with bright colors, it was the frequency of the exposure that mattered for memory.[12]

Calkins went on to be the first female president of both the American Psychological Association and American Philosophical Association, and studied under James, Münsterberg, and Edmund Sandford.

Her doctoral research was published in 1896 and the Department of Philosophy and Psychology at Harvard unanimously recommended that Calkins receive her PhD, having completed all coursework, examinations, and research for the degree. However, because Harvard did not accept women, Calkins was only allowed to take classes as a "guest" and was not officially recognized as a student. Harvard refused to grant her degree. (The most recent petition to award her a PhD from Harvard posthumously was denied in 2015.)

Calkins was clearly an important figure in the history of memory research. Yet, as cognitive psychologists and students of memory, we did not learn much, if anything, about her when we were in graduate school. For us, this is an important lesson: the history of our field is, like memory itself, not a perfect record of everything that has occurred. Rather, it is shaped and reconstructed by people with their own histories, relationships, and motives.

While functionalism can be seen as an alternative to structuralism, the two approaches were not irreconcilable.[13] The Gestalt school of psychology, on the other hand, outright rejected structuralism. Founded by Max Wertheimer, Kurt Koffka, and Wolfgang Köhler, Gestalt psychology emphasizes the importance of patterns and configurations in perception, "the whole is different than the sum of its parts". Gestalt psychology made many important contributions to our understanding of visual perception and problem solving, and we will use the gestalt concept of schema throughout this book (see Chapter 2).

Both gestalt and functionalism remain as useful approaches, with many of their terms and theories still being actively studied and modified. However, both approaches received a marked drop in consideration around the 1930s. In the early twentieth century, both were overshadowed by a much more prominent theory, another backlash to structuralism: behaviorism.

BEHAVIORISM

The most influential backlash to structuralism came in the form of behaviorism. Behaviorists advocated that if psychology was to advance as a scientific field, it should only focus on that which can be directly observed and measured: behavior. In this view, the mind became an unknowable black box. Input from stimuli in the environment went in, and output in the form of behavioral responses came out. Psychological theories were explained in stimulus-response chains that obviate the need to explain the mind. Memory, at least memory that relied on describing conscious experiences or perceptions, was not directly measurable and therefore could not be studied scientifically. Behaviorism was the next, and potentially biggest, twist in our history of memory research.

John Broadus Watson was behaviorism's founder and champion. At university he worked as a waiter at his boarding house, a janitor in the psychology department, and a caretaker in the animal laboratory of Henry Donaldson at the University of Chicago. There he received his PhD in 1903 from Donaldson and Angell. Watson taught at the University of Chicago, teaching courses on experimental psychology that used Titchener's manuals. By as early as 1904 he began having doubts as to the value of introspection, writing that he could "find out by watching their [rats] behavior everything that the other students are finding out by using human observers".[14(p. 276)] His mentor, Angell, disagreed with Watson's views on behaviorism, saying that "man is not a mere animal but a thinking being".[5(p. 403)]

Watson was eventually offered the position of chair of the psychology department at Johns Hopkins University in 1908. In taking on that position, he also inherited the editorship of the journal *Psychological Review*. There he published his behaviorist manifesto, *Psychology as the Behaviorist Views It*, in 1913.[15] He started researching children, concluding that children were not born with fears that had previously been considered "innate" like fear of the dark, snakes, etc. He surmised that fears must be learned, and set out to determine how these fears could be conditioned, famously studying "Little Albert".[16] Watson and his graduate student Rosalie Rayner exposed Little Albert to a white rat and other furry objects. Little Albert liked them at first, but after a while, they made very loud noises behind him while he was playing with the rat. Over time, Little Albert showed signs of fear toward the rat and furry objects.

Watson's behaviorism proved to be a very successful approach in experimental psychology. While it certainly helped that Watson himself held prominent positions (he served as president of the American Psychological Association in 1915), it also helped that behaviorism did, in fact, result in rigorous experiments that advanced our scientific understanding of human behavior and learning.

Watson had many prominent students and followers, but for the sake of space, we will highlight the most prominent, Burrhus Frederic Skinner. Skinner earned his PhD from Harvard in 1931. Skinner's landmark book, *The Behavior of Organisms*,[17] described his operant system of behavior. Skinner studied how animals *operate* in their environment to obtain rewards (usually food), thus terming this type of learning as operant conditioning. Are there certain schedules of rewards that lead to faster or more durable learning? What if the rewards stop—will the animal stop responding? These are the basic questions that Skinner's line of research set out to answer.

In 1951, Skinner described what he called shaping. Shaping is a method of animal learning where you take an already-occurring behavior and gradually reinforce the next approximation of the desired behavior, shaping one behavior into another. For example, a pig naturally roots around on the ground to find food. You can train a pig to roll a ball by shaping the rooting behavior into the new desired behavior. Similarly, Skinner used shaping to train a rat to drop a marble through a hole. Students named the rat Pliny the Elder, and *Life* magazine ran a feature on Skinner's "basketball-playing rat".[5] Skinner's most notable demonstration of shaping was *Project Orcon*—he trained pigeons to act as missile guidance systems. He was never able to convince the military to use pigeons, despite flawless performance in simulators.[5] Indeed, Skinner's principles of operant conditioning and shaping are now pervasive in animal training.

The first half of the twentieth century was marked by behaviorism in experimental psychology, restricting the number of experiments that could be conducted on memory. However, like the schools of thought that came before it, there was a growing consensus that behaviorism alone could not account for all human experiences.

THE COGNITIVE REVOLUTION

Behaviorism had relegated the mind to a black box—an unobservable and unmeasurable entity that could not be scientifically studied. However, not everyone abandoned the study of the mind. Frederic Bartlett was an English psychologist who grew up in the small town of Stow-on-the-Wold, England. He received his undergraduate degree in 1909 with a focus on logic. His master's degree was in ethics and sociology. He then started a second undergraduate degree in philosophy and psychology, and also dabbled in anthropology. The terms cognitive psychology and cognitive science were not used until the 1970s, but Bartlett's broad education and interest were very much in line with what we would consider cognitive science, an interdisciplinary field including psychology, linguistics, computer science, philosophy, anthropology, and neuroscience.

In memory research, Bartlett is remembered for his study using a version of the Native American folktale *War of the Ghosts*, which he published in 1932.[18] Bartlett had read Ebbinghaus's work with nonsense syllables and criticized the use of artificial stimuli that would not generalize to other memory phenomena. He wanted to study memory using more realistic materials. He chose *War of the Ghosts* because it had several elements that would be unfamiliar to the British participants who were asked to remember it. He found that these participants tended to make the same errors when recalling the story. For example, they consistently replaced *canoe* with *boat* in their recollection and changed *something black* coming out of the mouth to *foaming at the mouth*. Bartlett concluded that though the participants' recollection of the story was technically incorrect, they had the ability to understand the gist of the story and remember that (i.e., schemas, see Chapter 2). In other words, though they could not remember all of the parts, they largely remembered the whole of the story (a very Gestalt way of thinking about memory). Critically, he described the process of remembering the story as a process of *reconstruction*, rather than the mind simply reproducing a copy of a memory. Memory as a reconstructive process continues to be a central idea in memory research today.

In the mid-1950s, researchers interested in the mind began to pry open behaviorism's black box. This is often called the cognitive revolution. Important advances in the fields of linguistics, computer science, and neuroscience set the stage for the cognitive revolution. In linguistics, Noam Chomsky is one of the most important linguists of the twentieth century. Born to Ashkenazi Jewish immigrants in Philadelphia, Chomsky studied at the University of Pennsylvania and then Harvard, and started teaching at MIT in 1955. In 1957 Skinner published his book *Verbal Behavior*, which described language as any other type of learned material—learned over time through repeated associations.[19] Chomsky wrote a lengthy and harsh review of *Verbal Behavior*.[5] He argued that language is not learned merely by associations and repetitions. Instead, we humans seem to possess a unique predilection for grammar and structure. Chomsky's most well-known example for this is the sentence *Colorless green ideas sleep furiously*. Unless you have taken courses or read books in cognitive science, you are unlikely to have encountered this sentence. Further, it is complete nonsense. However, it fits the structure of English grammar, and you are therefore able to read it easily and understand the gist. If we were to violate the rules of grammar and rearrange the words, it becomes difficult to read, *Furiously sleep ideas green colorless*. Chomsky argues that the laws of learning as described by behaviorism do not account for your complex understanding of grammar that allow you to read completely novel and nonsensical sentences like *Colorless green ideas sleep furiously*.

The middle of the twentieth century also saw many exciting advances in computer science, most notably in the area of artificial intelligence (AI) and neuroscience. Computer scientists Allen Newell and Herbert Simon presented their work on the Logic Theory Machine, the first complete proof of a theorem ever carried out on a computing machine and an early precursor to AI.[20] By developing a computing machine that could complete complex proofs like humans, it was therefore possible to build thinking machines that could be used as models to study human thinking. Karl Spencer Lashley, an American psychologist with a PhD in genetics from Johns Hopkins University, criticized the behaviorist explanation of complex behaviors—like playing a piano or speaking a sentence. According to behaviorism, each complex behavior could be broken down into a series of simple behaviors which were themselves a matter of stimulus-response chains. Lashley argued that the mistakes people make in complex behaviors cannot be explained by a simple stimulus-response chain. For example, when typing on a keyboard, people often make mistakes that indicate they are thinking ahead. If you type *thses* instead of *these*, the only way you could type the *s* after the *h* is to know ahead of time that the *s* follows the *e*. Lashley proposed that memory and learning were distributed across the brain, allowing for a more flexible and robust system. His work was further refined by Donald Hebb, a Canadian who worked with Lashley during a brief stint at Harvard. Hebb explained the physiological mechanisms of learning in his 1949 book *Organization of Behavior*.[21] Hebb argued that learning happens at the level of the synapse, often encapsulated in the phrase "Cells that fire together, wire together".

George Miller is one of the cognitive psychologists most heavily associated with the cognitive revolution. He initially studied speech at the University of Alabama but was convinced by his psychology professor Donald Ramsdell to pursue psychology. Miller eventually went on to earn his PhD from Havard. Miller's famous paper, *The Magic Number 7*,[22] provided evidence that people can remember about seven things in their short-term memory. It is still one of the most cited works in memory research. Miller's other notable contribution to the cognitive revolution, in addition to influential writing, was that he taught Ulric Neisser, who went on to write the first textbook in cognitive psychology in 1967.[23]

MODERN MEMORY RESEARCH

By the 1970s, cognitive psychology had emerged as its own sub-discipline in psychology. While we can define psychology as the scientific study of the mind and behavior, we might define cognitive psychology as the scientific study of the mind *through* behavior. Though behaviorism made studying the mind somewhat unpopular for a period of time, cognitive psychologists (and psychologists more broadly), eventually began to use the rigorous experimental methods developed by behaviorists to make inferences about how the mind works. Modern memory research, as a sub-discipline within cognitive psychology and cognitive science, continues to use this approach. In 2004 Henry Roediger, president of the Association for Psychological Science, wrote in his presidential column, "In a very real sense, all psychologists today (at least those doing empirical research) are behaviorists. Even the most cognitively oriented experimentalists study behavior of some sort".[24] We will explore our modern understanding of memory—as a complex and multifaceted array of different types and systems—in Chapter 2.

This, however, is only one way to understand memory. While cognitive psychology is very much influenced by, and in turn influences, fields like neuroscience and educational psychology, it still remains its own discipline. Neuroscience is primarily concerned with structures in the brain and how they correspond to behaviors. Educational psychology research, generally, is much more applied and concerned with learning and memory in educational settings. Within the history of educational psychology, it shares common forerunners to cognitive psychology, like James and Thorndike. However, it was much more heavily influenced by developmental theories and applications to educational settings. Thus, while it shares a somewhat parallel history to cognitive psychology, educational psychology has a different set of methodologies and research questions. We will occasionally cite work from these related fields—at its core cognitive psychology is interdisciplinary—but we want to make it clear that is not our focus.

CONCLUSION: UNDERSTANDING THE PAST SERVES US IN UNDERSTANDING THE PRESENT AND FUTURE

Our understanding of memory, as cognitive psychologists, has been shaped by the history of the field. Thus, this history provides context about the lens through which we have studied memory, and how we explain memory within this book. This history is not a perfect record of everything that has ever happened related to the study of memory. While imperfect, this seems fitting; our own memories are not perfect records of the past. They are reconstructed given our current goals, and hopefully serve us well in the present and future.

2

TYPES OF MEMORY

As you learned in Chapter 1, the way researchers approach the study of memory has changed substantially from the early days of experimental psychology. Using rigorous behavioral experiments, researchers are able to make inferences about how memory works. What we have learned with these modern experimental and multidisciplinary techniques is that memory is extraordinarily complicated.[1] In 2008 Henry Roediger observed that "for 120 years, cognitive psychologists have sought general laws of learning and memory . . . none have stood the test of time".[2(p. 225)] Roediger goes on, "The fact that simple laws do not hold reveals the complex, interactive nature of memory phenomena".[2(p. 225)]

When we think of memory as the use of the past in service of the present and future, it becomes clear that there are many types of memory and memory processes. In fact, Endel Tulving, a famous memory researcher, suggested (perhaps jokingly) a list of 256 kinds of memory![3] We can remember the first time we met our partner, where we put our keys, running into a neighbor at the grocery store last week, or other past events big or small (episodic memory). But we can also remember general knowledge and concepts, like who was the first person on the moon or what the capital of Rhode Island is (semantic memory); remember how to do something, like riding a bike or typing (procedural memory); remember to do something in the future, like taking medications or remembering to take the pie out

DOI: 10.4324/9781003391166-2

of the oven (prospective memory); and remember things we are not consciously aware of, like the rules of our native language (implicit memory). Holding things in mind while we use them, like looking up a phone number on an Internet browser app and then typing it into the phone app, or remembering what a person just asked you while you form your response is also a form of memory (short-term or working memory). Memory is made up of a variety of different systems, and while they work together, we know from patients with brain damage and/or amnesia that the systems can operate at least somewhat independently (see Chapter 4).

In this chapter, we discuss different memory types and systems. The theme for this chapter, and really for the whole book, is that memory is more complex, spans more areas, and involves more nuance than people often think. The concepts introduced in this chapter are woven into the remaining chapters in the book. Figures 2.1 and 2.2 illustrate the different types of memories and systems covered in this chapter, and can help explain how they relate to one another.

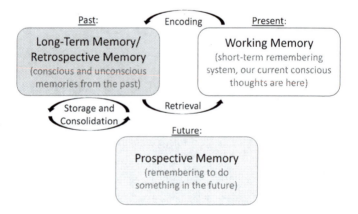

Figure 2.1 An illustration of the way our memory systems interact. Our long-term and working memory systems work together to allow the past to serve us in the present. Our memories for the future rely on both long-term and working memory.

Types of long-term, retrospective memories:

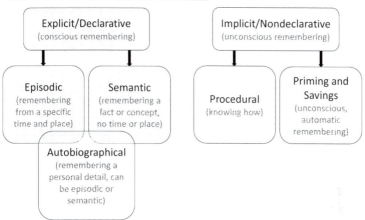

Figure 2.2 Different types of long-term, retrospective memories.

REMEMBERING IN THE SHORT AND LONG TERM

We use our memories both in the short and long term. A common misconception is that the difference between the two is simply a matter of time, perhaps a few hours compared to a few days or weeks. In fact, all of these delays would be considered long-term memory. Short-term remembering, called working memory, is actually much, much shorter than this. Our working memory only lasts approximately 15–30 seconds. And importantly, the distinction between working memory and long-term memory is not just a matter of time. Rather, they are thought to be different systems that work together.

The very short duration of working memory is often surprising to people. For example, can you remember any information about the quotes from the beginning of this chapter, without looking? Even if you have been reading the chapter in one sitting, the information from a couple of paragraphs ago, if remembered, is from your long-term memory system. Working memory is for holding information in mind while you are actively using it, and forgetting from this system happens extremely rapidly. Sometimes that information makes it into your long-term system, and sometimes you are able to retrieve information out of your long-term memory (i.e., *remember* it). If you do retrieve it, then you have brought it back into your working memory to say it, think about it, or use it in some way again. If you did not remember the quotes from the beginning of the chapter, this does not mean you have a "poor" memory. Your memory systems are working the way they should. You read the sentences, and as you were reading, you held the information in your working memory long enough to make sense of what you were reading. And then, as you continued to read, the words from those quotes were "lost" and replaced by new words from the page.

We use our working memories to maintain information in our conscious minds while we use it (or work with it). We can only hold so much information in our mind at once—imagine being on vacation with five friends in a new city, and trying to hold in mind dinner orders for six of you while remembering the directions to the restaurant and navigating there. Holding all of these things in mind is almost certainly beyond most people's working memory capacity, and writing some, or all, of this down would be advisable. We can only maintain information in our working memories for a few seconds unless we are actively attempting to keep them in our conscious awareness. Once we are no longer consciously holding information in working memory, we have to retrieve (i.e., remember) it from long-term memory to bring it back into our working memories.

Prior to the 1980s you would not find the term working memory in books or papers. Instead, you would find experiments and theories about short-term memory. Working memory is a more modern and updated understanding of short-term memory. Using the term short-term memory is outdated in research circles, and refers to a person's ability to remember static information, in order, for a few seconds. We can still measure a person's short-term memory span. Imagine I list off a series of numbers to you one at a time and then ask you to repeat them back to me in order (the digit span task). If you can successfully do this, then I would increase the number of digits that I present. For example:

$$8\text{-}5\text{-}2\text{-}6\text{-}9\text{-}1$$
$$5\text{-}2\text{-}1\text{-}9\text{-}6\text{-}3\text{-}8$$
$$2\text{-}5\text{-}4\text{-}9\text{-}8\text{-}5\text{-}2\text{-}7$$

Your memory span is the number of digits that you can accurately repeat back in order, and on average most people can remember seven plus or minus two.[4] But, as you can tell from the examples presented so far, we use our short-term remembering system for more than just keeping digits or other items in mind in order.

In the 1980s Alan Baddeley reconceptualized this short-term system and called it working memory.[5] His model originally contained three different systems. The phonological loop stores auditory information; it is responsible for one's ability to complete the digit span task and rehearse other verbal information. The visuospatial sketchpad maintains visual and spatial information. The central executive is essentially our attention system that controls the other systems and controls our ability to switch attention between tasks, manipulate information, and manage distractions. Later, Baddeley added another component called the episodic buffer, which is thought to temporarily store anything retrieved from long-term episodic memory (discussed in the next section of this chapter) and to coordinate overlap in auditory and visual information.

Long-term memory, on the other hand, is our memory for things that are no longer being held in our conscious awareness. The term is essentially used for every type of memory that is not part of working memory.[6] Thus, long-term memory is a vast concept that can be divided up many different ways. In the remaining sections of this chapter, we will attempt to explain various types of long-term memory. But first, we will explain a few basic terms that apply broadly to long-term memory.

There are three general stages of memory; and, while each stage is not perfectly distinct from the others, it is still useful to understand the terms for each stage and what they generally represent. Encoding is the initial acquisition of a memory. It can involve reading, listening, experiencing, or even imagining something. Once a memory is encoded, it is stored and consolidated. We store representations of our memories with various features. However, as you will learn throughout this book, our memory representations are rarely perfect. The representations are consolidated during sleep, making them more stable and durable.[7] Retrieval is the process of remembering. When we retrieve a memory that has been stored, we reconstruct that memory, bringing it into our working memory (i.e., conscious awareness). Importantly, retrieval is not like opening a file from a filing cabinet. Instead, we reconstruct our memories based on the cues that are available when we retrieve them, and the features that were stored as part of the memory. This reconstruction process can be incomplete or even involve modifications or additions that were not a part of the original memory. In a TED Talk, Elizabeth Loftus said,

> Many people believe that memory works like a recording device.... But decades of work in psychology has shown that this just is not true. Our memories are constructive. They are reconstructive. Memory works a little bit more like a Wikipedia page; you can go in there and change it, but so can other people.[8](04:56)

REMEMBERING DIFFERENT TYPES OF INFORMATION

Explicit memory (also called declarative memory) refers to consciously retrieved long-term memories. (We will cover unconscious remembering, or nondeclarative memory, in the next section.) We can further break explicit memory into two different types: episodic and semantic memory.

Episodic memory is our memory for personal experiences, or "episodes". We can have episodic memories for events that are big and small. I (Megan) remember my wedding very well, and also remember how my husband and I spent our fifth wedding anniversary—we spent the entire day in the hospital, and I delivered our daughter that evening! (Our anniversary belongs to her now.) I can also remember chatting with a colleague last week, and feeling tired the last time I went to Target. These are all my own personal experiences, and my subjective experience is *remembering* them. When we remember episodic memories, we travel back in our minds to a specific time and place.[6, 9] By this definition, episodic memories need not feel particularly personal. For example, in the research laboratory, we may ask participants to read a list of words, like *elephant, cucumber, soap, brake, marriage*, and so on. Then, after some time passes, we can ask participants to think back to the list and write down as many of the words as they can remember. We are not asking the participants to remember what the words mean, though thinking about the meaning of the words would likely help their memory for the words. Instead, we are asking them to think back to a specific time and place, namely a few minutes ago in the lab when they read the list, and recall what was on that list. In that way, if the participant writes *elephant*, it is an episodic memory but unlikely to feel very personal to them.

Semantic memory is our basic knowledge of the world. Semantic memory includes things like knowing what an elephant is, knowing that fire trucks tend to be red, and knowing that Sydney is in Australia. The subjective experience here is *knowing* and specifically does not include any specific time or place details.[6] Our semantic memory is organized such that related concepts are associated with one another, like doctor and nurse, or colors like green, blue, and yellow. Because they are associated in our minds, when we think about one, the other is activated in our semantic network.

Our experiences also help us create schemas.[6] A schema is a framework that we use to help organize our knowledge. For example, imagine that you are going out to eat at a new restaurant this weekend that just opened. You probably do not need to learn how to behave in this restaurant as if it were a new experience, even though you have never been there. Instead, you likely have a restaurant schema, based on your past experiences in restaurants, that will help you navigate the situation. Your restaurant schema is probably rich with detail, with slightly different scripts for fast-food restaurants and sit-down restaurants. This schema helps you transfer what you learned from past restaurant experiences to the new restaurant this weekend. We also have schemas for things like the order of events when you visit the library (when there is a very specific order, we call this a script), what a nurse looks like (our schema for nurse could be a stereotype), and what a dorm room typically contains.

Autobiographical memory, or memories for one's personal history, is yet another type of memory.[6] Because episodic memories are memories for events we have experienced, many episodic memories are also autobiographical. These include things like remembering your first day of school, your wedding, or meeting your child for the first time. However, not all episodic memories are autobiographical; remembering *elephant* from a word list does not really rise to the level of a personal detail. Further, autobiographical memories can also be semantic. Knowing one's passport number or wedding anniversary date would be considered autobiographical semantic memories. I also know specific details about when and where I was born. Of course, neither of these memories involve my own mental time travel back to the specific time and place, even though I know the specific time and place.

Episodic and semantic memory are not perfectly distinct categories. There are certainly times when the lines blur between episodic and semantic memory. For example, most people know that up until very recently (2022), Queen Elizabeth II was the Queen of England. Many also likely know that she was the longest-serving monarch in British history. Some who were old enough at the time may remember when she became queen in 1952, but because this was over seven decades ago, most will not have a specific episodic memory for these events. Rather, most of us just know Elizabeth II was the Queen, making these memories semantic in nature. It is certainly possible to have episodic memories related to her (for example, we have an episodic memory for visiting Buckingham Palace briefly after a teacher-training workshop in London), but the general memory *Elizabeth II was Queen* is likely semantic. However, most people also likely know that her son,

Charles III, is, as of this writing, King. And, because his coronation was somewhat recent, many more people are likely to remember the coronation or other events surrounding when he took the throne. A person might remember watching the coronation on TV or gathering in the streets of London. Thus, the memory *Charles III is King* could easily be episodic in nature for many people if it causes them to think back to a specific time and place and recall details about his becoming king. These time and place features are a part of the memory, and are a part of what is recalled, making the memory more episodic in nature. As we move further and further away from the events surrounding his coronation, the likelihood that *Charles III is King* is an episodic memory for some becomes smaller as those time and place features tend to be forgotten. For others, however, cues to think about the King of England might evoke episodic memories that involve time and place features for a long time. Thus the degree to which a memory is episodic or semantic depends on the features that a person is recalling when they are remembering an event.

Episodic, semantic, and autobiographical memories tend to fall in the broad category of explicit memory, or instances of conscious recollection. When you travel back to a moment within your memory, like your wedding day or that the word *elephant* occurred on a list that you read, or indicate that you know a fact, like *Charles III is King*, you are remembering in a conscious way. In the next section of this chapter, we cover the differences between conscious and unconscious remembering.

CONSCIOUS AND UNCONSCIOUS REMEMBERING

Our broad definition of memory, the use of the past in service of the present and future, leaves room for both conscious and unconscious remembering. It is very possible for past information or experiences to affect the present or future without conscious awareness. For example, I (Megan) occasionally teach an upper-level research methods class that students take during or near the final year of their undergraduate psychology program, and can only be taken after completion of two prerequisite research methods courses. Thus, this course builds upon a great deal of prior knowledge that students should have learned previously. Of course, we know from research on memory and our own experiences that just because we learned something does not mean that we remember it indefinitely. I cannot tell you how many times I have heard the phrase "We never learned that before". It is possible that certain topics, such as factorial inter-actions, were not covered in previous courses taught by some profes-sors, or that the student was absent from class and missed the topic. However, what I think is much more likely is that the student does not have a conscious memory for learning the topic, and the topic feels somewhat unfamiliar to them. Upon discussing factorial interactions in our class, some students are able to grasp the concept more quickly than would be typical for a student who has never been exposed to the idea. Their past learning about factorial interactions is helping them grasp the concept more quickly, even though it is happening uncon-sciously. Their savings in relearning (as studied by Ebbinghaus,[10] see Chapter 1) allows for this type of unconscious remembering.

Researchers use a few terms to distinguish between conscious and unconscious memories. For example, explicit memory (or declara-tive memory) refers specifically to conscious remembering whereas implicit memory (or nondeclarative memory) involves prior expe-riences affecting performance on a task without conscious aware-ness.[6] In the laboratory, an explicit memory test is one where the participant is given a cue to recall or recognize something. In the last section, we gave an example of free recall, an explicit memory test, where participants were given a list of words and were then asked to write down as many words as they could remember from that list. Implicit tests do not involve a cue to consciously remember. For example, in the laboratory, participants may be presented with a list of words (e.g., *elephant, marriage, soap, brake, cucumber*) and then later are given "puzzles" to solve, such as thinking of the first word that comes to mind when given a word stem like *br____*. Participants are not asked to think back to the list, but if participants who saw *brake* are more likely to complete the stem with *brake*, as opposed to *bread*, *brother*, or *brain*, then this indicates that their past experience with the list is shaping the present. In cognitive psychology, this is often called priming. The idea is that seeing (or hearing) a word, like *brake*, activates our representation of that concept in our semantic network (our network of learned concepts and how they are related to one another). It is like bringing the concept more closely to the front of our minds, and so when the opportunity arises, we are more likely to think of that word, or other words that are related. For example, after seeing (or hearing) the word *brake*, a person might be more likely to think about cars, mechanics, or bicycles.

Procedural memory is a form of unconscious memory because we often learn a procedure, like tying our shoes or riding a bike, and then continue to utilize those past experiences unconsciously when we perform the procedures later. Think about learning to tie your shoes as a young child. When we first learn to do this, each step feels difficult and requires a lot of thought. However, as we practice over time, we tend to get better at tying our shoes, and the process becomes swift, effortless, and, importantly, unconscious. Once we know how to tie our shoes, it actually becomes difficult to consciously think about the procedure. In fact, if we needed to teach someone to tie their shoes now, we would need to grab a shoe and do it ourselves in order to see the steps and begin to break them down in a way that we could explain to another person, something we both certainly will be doing when our young children get a little bit older. Procedural memories often refer to motor skills, but some have conceptualized them as referring to mental procedures as well, such as multiplying two numbers.[6]

The distinction between conscious and unconscious memory does not map perfectly onto intentional and unintentional remembering (or voluntary vs. involuntary remembering). Certainly, unconscious memories are unintentional; by definition, intentionally retrieving a memory means that it must be a conscious process. However, conscious memories can also be unintentional. For example, a friend could ask me (Megan) about my trip to Brisbane, Australia, in

January 2020. I could then intentionally think back to the trip and share a story about holding koalas at the Koala Sanctuary (it was as cute as it sounds). However, I could also find myself picking up toys around the house and notice the stuffed koala that my husband and I purchased for our son while we were there. This could cause me to think about holding the koalas and picking out the toy for him. Memories can also seem to pop into one's head out of the blue, and those would also be involuntary memories, albeit conscious ones.

Similar to the distinction between semantic and episodic memory discussed in the previous section, the lines between conscious and unconscious procedural memories, and between procedural memories and other types of memories, can sometimes blur. Take the example of teaching someone to tie a shoe. If a person is consciously executing the *tying a shoe* procedure in order to teach another person, the procedure has become conscious. Does this mean tying one's shoe is no longer a procedural memory? If not, what type of memory would it be? As another example, imagine a surgeon in their final year of medical residency (i.e., medical training that typically follows medical school). As a surgeon with practice, they should be able to go through a common procedure within their specialty, such as a cesarean section on a pregnant person, without much conscious thought about the steps. Thus, the cesarean section is a procedural memory to them. However, if they have a brand-new intern in their first year of residency in the operating room with them, the experienced surgeon should also be able to articulate what they are doing and why, as if each step is a semantic memory (or memory for facts). And importantly, doing so is conscious. Textbooks can articulate the steps involved in a cesarean section as well, though, of course, a surgeon in training really needs some hands-on instruction and practice to learn. Is a cesarean section a procedural memory in some cases but a string of semantic memories in other cases? One could argue that surgical skills are complicated and thus can have features of both semantic and procedural memories (and likely episodic memories, too). But either way, it seems that the boundaries of these categories are not perfect.

Finally, unconscious remembering, and specifically implicit memory tests, are historically linked to the study of amnesia (see Chapter 4). While many have the general understanding that amnesic patients have trouble with their memories, we know from an experiment by Elizabeth Warrington and L. Weiskrantz[11] that memory deficits for amnesic patients can vary largely on how memory is tested. In their experiment with very severe amnesic patients, when asked to explicitly recall information, like words from a list, the amnesia patients showed much lower performance than control participants without memory problems. However, when they were tested implicitly, the deficits disappeared. This suggests that even very severe amnesic patients can encode new information or events, but they can struggle with active retrieval.

REMEMBERING FOR THE FUTURE

Memory is not just about the past. Arguably, one of the more useful aspects of memory is our ability to remember to do something in the future. And, by the same token, forgetting to do something that you were supposed to do is one of the more frustrating occurrences. Memory for intentions to be performed in the future is called prospective memory. I need to remember to cancel the subscription before we get charged again; I need to remember to take dinner out of the oven after 35 minutes; I need to remember to take my medication every 24 hours; I need to remember to pick up the dry cleaning on the way home from work this week. These are all examples of prospective memory.

We can contrast prospective memory with retrospective memory, or remembering the past. Of course, prospective memory still has some retrospective features. For example, imagine it is Sunday evening and you decide you want to watch a specific documentary. You discover you can watch it on a streaming platform that has a free 7-day trial. You sign up and learn that once the trial ends you will be charged for the subscription. You think, *In 6 days I should cancel the subscription.* This is a prospective memory because you need to remember to execute your intention, to cancel, after a certain amount of time. After 6 days, hopefully, you remember to cancel the subscription, or at least evaluate your options. If you remember, then you must be remembering your intention, which occurred in the past (retrospective). You may even remember signing up for the free trial, or aspects of the documentary that you watched last Sunday, which would all be retrospective episodic memories. Still, because the intention was created, memory researchers classify this as prospective memory.

Prospective memory comes in two general forms: event-based and time-based. An event-based prospective memory involves remembering to do something when a specific event occurs, like remembering to pick up the dry cleaning on the way home from work. A time-based prospective memory involves remembering to do something after a specific amount of time or on a specific schedule, like remembering to take medication every 24 hours or remembering to take dinner out of the oven after 35 minutes.

Time-based prospective memories can be more difficult to remember in general than event-based prospective memories because there is not an event-based cue to help trigger the memory. Time keeps ticking on, and we either remember to do the thing when a certain amount of time has passed or we do not. With event-based prospective memories, there is an event tied to the prospective memory, and the event can serve as a cue to help us remember our intention. Thus, one strategy to help increase success of remembering our time-based prospective memory is to turn it into an event-based prospective memory. Most of us do this all the time without even realizing it. For example, when most of us put dinner in the oven, we do not just rely on our own ability to watch the clock. Instead, we set a timer. Now we have an event-based prospective memory that is much easier; when the oven timer goes off, we need to remember to take dinner out of the oven. Similarly, it is a good idea to set up some sort of calendar reminder to cancel the free trial if that is your intention. If the technology pushes an alert to you without having to check your calendar, then that is even better!

Still, even event-based prospective memories are not foolproof. Changes to our routine or event-based prospective memories that are not part of our normal day-to-day can be difficult to remember. You may have heard about accidental deaths of children because they were left in the car for long periods of time. It certainly is not the most common cause of death in children; but still, in the United States, 40 children on average die from heatstroke in a car from being left or getting trapped.[12] Forty children per year is 40 more than we want, and for those families the prospective memory error is horrific. Most people think they could never forget something so important, or have a hard time imagining doing so because getting their child out of the car seems like such an important part of a routine. It seems to most people like a problem they would never have. But as memory researchers, we can see how easy it would be for any parent to make this fatal error.

Imagine that on normal days you drop your oldest child off at school on your way to work, and your partner drops off your youngest. However, your partner was out of town over the weekend and was unexpectedly delayed; it is Monday morning and you are flying solo. The morning is hectic and you leave the house late, resulting in heavier traffic than usual. You have a busy day today, and so you are mentally rearranging your morning to figure out how you will get everything done. You drop off your oldest like you always do, and then automatically head toward your office like you always do. You forget that your youngest is napping quietly in their car seat. You park, grab your bag, and hustle into the office. This is every parent's worst nightmare but is preventable with a good event-based memory cue. Every time you buckle your children into their car seats, leave something essential in the back with them, like your purse or briefcase, or even a shoe. Do this every time so that it is routine. This way, when you park your vehicle, you will have to go to the back seat, where your kids are, to retrieve the item. This is not to say your bag or shoe is more important to you than your kids. Of course not! But by creating an event-based prospective memory cue that you cannot miss, you will be able to remember to check for those precious little ones even when you would not normally have them with you.

CONCLUSION: MEMORY IS COMPLEX

Memory is not just a collection of past events. It is more varied and multifaceted than most people realize, with different types of memory and memory systems. These memory types are not perfectly distinct, and classifying all memories as one type of memory or another is not always possible. Still, understanding the different types of memories, and the features that we encode with those memories, can help you understand memory as a whole. Functionally, our memory systems allow us to use the past in service of the present and future. Thus, our memories from the past influence our present and future. For example, people who are depressed often have difficulty both remembering past and imagining future positive life experiences.[13] Our ability to imagine the future and act in the present depends, in part, on how we remember the past. People with different pasts— different life experiences than your own—will thus act differently in the present and imagine their futures differently from you. By better understanding the complexity and nuance of our memory systems, we better understand all of the ways in which memory affects our everyday lives.

3

MEMORY THROUGH THE LIFESPAN

If you are the parent or caretaker of a young child, you almost certainly have found yourself watching the same shows repeatedly for days on end, and are unlikely to forget this experience (or the shows). Yet the children will not necessarily remember this when they are older. Like many children, we both had our repeat shows. For Megan it was *The Wizard of Oz*, and for Althea it was either *My Little Pony: The Movie* or *The Care Bears Movie*. Althea is not sure, helping make this point! We both have vague memories, if any memory at all, of watching these movies on repeat but, in the past, have been assured by our parents that it happened extremely frequently. We both hardly remember something that happened repeatedly, yet we could tell so many stories from our college days, seemingly with great detail and accuracy (though who knows how accurate the memories really are). Is the difference just that in one case we were children, in the other adults? Is it that one happened longer ago than the other?

The complex nature of memory becomes even more so when we consider memory across our lifespan, because memory does not function the exact same way our whole lives. As we age, our memory systems change. Most people have a general sense of how memory changes over time: memory is best during early adulthood and worst during our youngest and oldest years. While this is generally true, it is

DOI: 10.4324/9781003391166-3

a bit more complicated than that. In this chapter, we discuss memory across the lifespan from childhood to early and later adulthood.

CHILDHOOD MEMORY

What is your earliest memory from childhood? Most people cannot remember much from their early years. You may be able to remember some things from elementary or primary school, but certainly not as much as you remember from young adulthood. And it is not just the details that we seem to forget. Large events or even things that happened repeatedly, like watching a movie 100 times, can be forgotten. However, just because we do not have many memories from childhood does not mean our memory systems are completely undeveloped in childhood. If I (Althea) mention in front of my 3-year-old that we can go to the playground later today, he will not forget; he will ask about the playground repeatedly until we go. However, he does not remember much from day-to-day and rarely describes events that occurred months ago.

When we ask about childhood memory, we really could be asking one of two larger sets of questions. One is, how much can children remember in the moment or from day-to-day, as children? How does memory function in childhood? When an event happens, how long will a child remember it (episodic memory)? If a child learns what a dog is, will they retain their memory for this concept (semantic memory)? Once a kid learns how to do something, like roll over or crawl, do they retain these procedural memories? The other set is, how much of these memories do we retain into adulthood? How much do we remember from childhood? Certainly, we remember how to walk, wave, and clap. We remember concepts that we have learned. But how much of our episodic memories do we retain?

MEMORY IN CHILDHOOD

Like everything else, children's memory systems develop as they grow, so they do not function the same way as adults' memory systems.

Some memory systems develop rapidly and quite early. For example, some research shows that fetuses can recognize their mother's voice 1–2 weeks before birth.[1] Very young infants develop procedural memories, like learning how to roll over. Further, in the first year of life, babies develop many semantic memories—like learning what a dog is, or who their caretakers are. However, assessing whether very young children's memories are implicit or explicit, and assessing episodic memories when children are less verbal, is very difficult.

Infants can learn from a single event and maintain that information for some time. Because infants cannot verbalize what they can remember, researchers have used creative tasks to test their memory instead. For example, in one task, researchers tied a ribbon to an infant's foot and attached a mobile to the other end.[2] They measured how long it took the baby to learn that when they kick their feet the mobile moves. Then, the researchers waited a certain amount of time (e.g., a few hours, days, or weeks) and again attached the ribbon to the baby's foot. Because babies are interested in the movement of the mobile, if they remembered their previous experience, they would immediately start kicking their feet, and it would be faster compared to control infants who had not been exposed to the mobile and ribbon before. If they forgot about it, then it would take some time for them to relearn that kicking makes the mobile move, and would be similar to control infants. Using this task and similar tasks, researchers have shown that infants can remember for weeks, depending on the exact age of the infant. Researchers have also shown some parallels between childhood memory and adult memory. For example, when the infants are exposed to the ribbon and mobile twice, they will remember for longer if the two exposures were spaced out in time compared to massed very close together[3] (see spaced practice in Chapter 6).

However, assessing childhood episodic memories becomes complicated. Take the example of the infants learning that when they kick with a ribbon tied to their foot, they can move a mobile. Through their behavior, kicking quickly when put in the same situation again, they show evidence of retaining that past experience. Thus, we can confidently say they have memory ability. But are they consciously remembering the past experience, as would be required to demonstrate episodic memory? Or have they simply learned an association? In other words, we do not know whether their memory is explicit or implicit. Because they cannot verbalize what they are thinking, we cannot ask them whether they have a conscious awareness of the memory.

Researchers believe that around the time children are preschool aged, they begin developing their ability to use other memory systems. By 4 years old, children are able to hold 2–3 items in their working memory; however, children do not rehearse information in the same way as adults until they are about 7 years old.[4] As children continue to age, their ability to retain and manipulate information in their minds increases, and their ability to do so can affect their ability to learn new things.[5]

Importantly, around 2 or 3 years old, children begin developing their ability to recall episodic memories, or events from their past. However, very young children tend to be generally poor at recalling past events relative to adults. This does not mean young children cannot remember anything. As with adults, it is possible that children have enhanced memory of highly emotional events, such as an emergency room visit.[6, 7] For example, in one study, Carole Peterson and Nikki Whalen interviewed children 2–13 years old 5 years after a medical emergency that required hospital treatment.[7] The children had relatively accurate recall of the events. Even the 2-year-olds had accurate recall of the event, though they recalled less than the older children did. Children, like adults, appear more likely to remember details, especially central details, about an emotional event[6, 7] (see Chapter 5). A rare exception to this is eidetic memory, or remembering information nearly perfectly.[8] While eidetic memory is rare, it is more often seen in children than in adults (see Chapter 4).

How parents discuss past events with their children is related to how children remember the events. For example, Minda Tessler and Katherine Nelson tested the memories of 3.5-year-olds who attended a museum with their mothers one week earlier.[9] They found that the children could remember some of the details, and this was especially true if the mothers had discussed the event with their children. In another medical emergency experiment very similar to the one described earlier, researchers assessed the memories of children 2–5 years old both a few days and 2 years after an emergency room visit due to an injury.[6] On average, the older children in the study remembered more than the younger children. In addition, when the children's parents engaged in more elaborative conversation with them, encouraging them to continue discussing the event and adding details, the children also tended to remember more.

Thus, young children begin to develop episodic memories as toddlers and preschoolers, and these memory systems seem to improve with age. Still, under most circumstances, most children show lower rates of remembering past events than adults, even for things that occurred in the relatively recent past.[10] This suggests that memories do not form in the same way during early childhood as they do later in childhood and into adulthood. In addition, once the person reaches adulthood, they are unlikely to be able to recall many of these episodic memories, the topic of the next section in this chapter.

MEMORY FROM CHILDHOOD

When we ask an adult what their earliest memory is, we are almost certainly interested in episodic memories. You are likely completely uninterested in the fact that we can still roll and crawl around on the floor (Megan confirmed this recently playing with her daughter). As we have already discussed, we retain many procedural and semantic memories from early childhood (e.g., we also still know that a pig says "oink"). This is not what tends to interest people about someone's memories. Instead, when most people ask about your earliest memory, they want to know about the earliest event in your life that you can remember, your earliest episodic autobiographical memory.

Most evidence suggests that while some adults may have sparse memories from their very early years, we largely do not maintain many episodic memories from early childhood into adulthood.[10] The finding that we have very few, if any, memories of events from very early ages (0–3 years old) is called infantile amnesia. There are, however, some studies demonstrating memory for emotional or stressful events that seem to contradict infantile amnesia. For example, in the medical emergency studies discussed in the previous section, children as young as 2 years old were able to remember details of their injury 2–5 years later.[6, 7] Still, these were highly emotional and stressful events, the children could not remember every detail, and, importantly, they were regularly reminded about the events which likely strengthened their memory for the events.[7] Childhood memories from between 2–5 years old are relatively rare.[4] Yet you may have heard someone claiming to remember events from very early childhood, maybe even from before 2 years old, maybe even with great detail. So what about these very early childhood memories that some people seem to have? How often are these memories real or accurate?

We can use an example to illustrate a few points about memory in general, and memories for early childhood experiences. I (Megan) have a memory of an injury from when I was approximately 10 months old. According to my memory, my mom was heating pureed baby food for me on the stove while holding me. The food overheated quickly and splattered on my hand. My mom and grandma took me to the emergency room. The doctors questioned them repeatedly, bandaged me up, and sent us home. My dad arrived home from work, saw my hand in a big bandage, and asked, "What happened?!".

This event is real, but there are some details of my memory that are not correct. My mom was not heating baby food on the stove in a pot; she heated a small jar in the microwave. (This makes a lot more sense.) The food did not heat evenly, and when she stirred it, it splattered onto my hand. I am also missing some details. My grandparents met us at our house, and when we left for the emergency room, my mom backed into my grandfather's car! (in her defense, there was minimal damage and I was screaming *very* loudly).

Memory errors like these are completely normal.[11] My most glaring error, and the giveaway that this is not an authentic memory from the event itself, is the setting. When I think about this memory I can see us in the kitchen. I can see myself crawling to the door, and my dad walking in after work. The problem? I am imagining the wrong kitchen. I was just under 1 when this happened, but we moved when I was about 4. I cannot remember the first house at all, but I do remember the next house, where I lived from 4–18 years old, very well. This detail tells me that I have heard this story as retold by others, and I was able to imagine the events in the only kitchen that I could remember.

Essentially, I am committing a source error, or a misattribution.[11] A source error is any time we misremember the source of an original event. Did you read about an event in a reputable newspaper or on an acquaintance's social media page? Did the instructor explain this in class, or did you read about it in a textbook? Did something really happen, or did you just imagine it? When we imagine something, we engage in mental processing. There is encoding that happens. At the time of retrieval, we can mistake an imagined event for one that happened. I am clearly mistaking an authentic memory of an event from my infancy with imagining it happening based on hearing the story.

Source memory errors present a big problem with determining whether we can form memories of events from very early childhood. We certainly can know about things that happened to us at a very young age, and we can imagine them or even view pictures of them. Our memories might be accurate, close to accurate, or even only partially correct, and all of this would be normal. But that does not mean we have a memory of the actual event itself.

The example earlier demonstrates that evaluating our own memories from early childhood is complicated, and, like with all memory, having high confidence and recalling a lot of details does not mean the memory is accurate. Most adults' earliest memories are from 3 or more years old, with an estimated range of 2–8 years old.[4] We know from the previous section in this chapter that children can remember their past, recalling events prior to 3 years old as they did in the medical emergency studies.[6,7] Yet, by the time we reach adulthood, these memories are most often no longer recallable. It would be a mistake to assume that our childhood memories simply fade and are eventually forgotten over time; if that were the case, then as adults continue to age, we would expect their earliest memories to get later and later into childhood. However, this does not typically happen. My (Althea) earliest memories have remained my earliest memories throughout adulthood. At 27 years old I could remember a few things from when I was about 4 years old (namely the birth of my younger sister), and I can still remember those things from when I was about 4 years old now at 37 years old. I have not forgotten these memories in the last 10 years; my earliest memories did not shift from when I was 4 years old to when I was 14 years old. It is possible that a failure to recall events from very early childhood as adults is due to those memories being inaccessible for explicit recall.[12] Whatever the reason, when a person claims to remember something from infancy, it is unlikely to be an authentic memory from the event itself.

From when we are about 5 or 6 years old, the volume of memories we retain into adulthood dramatically increases. Further, our memories for events that occur later in childhood are also much more likely to be integrated into existing knowledge structures, and the meaning of events becomes increasingly important. We are able to remember more and more, with a dramatic peak in what we remember from late adolescence to early adulthood (roughly 16–25 years old), called the reminiscence bump. To study this, researchers gave adults cue words and asked them to recall the first memories that came to mind. Certainly, many of the memories came from the relatively recent past, such as something that happened last week or within the last year. But when memories were reported from the past, a large number came from late adolescence and early adulthood. Interestingly, this effect occurs across cultures,[13] suggesting there is something special about this time frame for remembering, whether it be because our encoding systems are at their peak performance at this time, or important shifts in developing our identity tend to occur during these years.

MEMORY IN ADULTHOOD

In early adulthood, we experience our cognitive peak. Some abilities peak later than others, but generally, the peak and subsequent decline of various cognitive abilities happens earlier than many of us think (or want to believe). Processing speed, the ability to take in, integrate, and respond to information, including encoding and retrieving memories, peaks around 20 years old, and working memory ability peaks around 30 years old.[14] We all know that aging comes with some cognitive decline. Reduction in memory ability is one of the most frequent complaints mentioned by older adults and is one of the more feared results of aging.[15, 16] Given that life expectancy in 2019 was over 80 years in the United Kingdom and Canada and in the upper 70s in the United States,[17] the average person spends many more years past their cognitive peak than leading up to it. Is it all downhill after we turn 30? Not exactly. Some aspects of memory improve during typical aging. Vocabulary peaks anywhere from one's 40s to even 60s or early 70s.[14] Relatedly, general knowledge can remain the same or even increase with aging.

Memory is complex and spans many areas, and not all facets of memory change in the same way as we age. Processing speed and working memory abilities tend to decline after young adulthood. Episodic memory performance tends to decline as well; older adults typically perform more poorly than younger adults on tasks that require episodic memory, such as remembering items from a list or remembering what was read from a text passage.[16] In general, age-related declines start small but become more rapid in later adulthood, around approximately the mid-70s.[16] But even within these general areas, not all abilities decline exactly the same way. Working memory is an example. Older adults tend to perform as well as younger adults with memory span tasks (see Chapter 2); they can maintain about the same number of digits in their working memory, typically seven plus or minus two items.[16] However, when a working memory task requires greater work from the central executive, such as directing one's attention, managing two competing tasks, and/or more active processing or manipulation of information, then on average, older adults show deficits compared to younger adults.[18]

Semantic memory tends to remain the same, or even increase, with age. Older adults can typically perform as well as younger adults in the retention of facts and general knowledge. Vocabulary performance can be the same or better for older adults compared to younger adults. Procedural memory tends to be preserved with age as well. However, again, the story is a bit more nuanced than this. Remembering semantic knowledge does not appear to decline during healthy aging when older adults are given plenty of time to remember. However, accessing semantic memories can sometimes be more challenging for older adults; they report more blocks when trying to remember proper names and are slower in accessing the stored information.[19] When tasks have a time limit, older adults often perform worse than younger adults, likely due to processing speed declines.

Of course, predicting how any given individual will experience memory changes with age is even more complicated. Cognitive aging research focuses more on the average performance of individuals of different ages rather than following the performance of an individual as they age. Further, people can differ from one another in more ways than just age, and these other individual differences can affect the ways in which our memory abilities change with healthy aging.[20, 21] Factors such as health, education, lifestyle activity, environmental support, genetics, and others can all affect how memory performance changes with age.

One individual factor that can have a large, though not necessarily permanent, effect on memory performance is sleep.[22] Losing even small amounts of sleep can lead to sleep deprivation and declines in cognitive function.[23] Further, we cannot simply consume caffeine to bring our cognitive functioning back to our best, and there is no reliable evidence that caffeine has a positive effect on memory ability.[24] (This fact is truly unfortunate for us, and surely many readers.) Aging itself is related to changes in sleep duration and quality.[25] There are also big life events that can affect sleeping behaviors, and some of these tend to happen at predictable times in the lifespan. For example, having a baby typically leads to sleep deprivation, and very often happens during our "peak cognitive functioning years" (i.e., 20s, 30s, or very early 40s; of course, this is not always the case, and we know that a person can become a new parent or caregiver at any age).

Thus, especially for those first few months, cognitive functioning and memory performance may be worse than a few years down the line. Certainly, there are other reasons to lose sleep, and other life events can also cause more temporary changes in cognitive performance, such as loss and grief.[26] Fluctuations in memory performance like these are a normal part of life. Of course, we should all try to maintain healthy sleep habits to avoid sleep deprivation, which can happen with even small amounts of sleep loss, whenever possible. As mothers of young children, we are very aware that this is not always possible.

Experiencing memory declines can be scary and frustrating; memory is used in so many areas of our lives. Up to this point in the chapter, we have discussed changes in memory during healthy aging. Unfortunately, some loss in memory ability is just a part of getting older. But an added fear for many is that memory loss could be a sign of more serious cognitive decline, namely dementia or Alzheimer's disease.

Several different diseases can cause dementia, affecting approximately 55 million people globally, and they are characterized by memory loss and changes to thinking and social abilities.[27] Alzheimer's disease is the most common subtype of dementia, and is characterized by progressive memory loss and other cognitive deficits (e.g., thinking, reasoning, making decisions, etc.). The disease typically starts with smaller memory lapses, such as forgetting events or conversations, or difficulty finding the word for an object. As the disease progresses, the memory loss continues to become more severe and affects the person's ability to function in their daily lives. There is currently no cure for Alzheimer's disease, but there are medications that can slow the progression of symptoms, especially if started early.[28] Caretakers can also help by creating a safe environment that supports the person with Alzheimer's disease. For example, installing alarm sensors in the home and keeping important valuables in one common location can help.

It is important to remind everyone that lapses in memory are extremely common. This book is filled with examples of imperfect memory! Healthy aging involves decreases in memory performance.

With Alzheimer's disease, these memory lapses are persistent and get worse over time. Of course, given that medications are more effective when action is taken early, it is a good idea to speak to your health-care provider, or offer to help a friend or family member speak to their health-care provider, if you are concerned about yourself or a loved one.

CONCLUSION: MEMORY CHANGES AS WE AGE

From fond childhood memories to cherished life events that we take with us into later adulthood, memory plays a key role in our development and aging—and development and aging affect our memory processes. Memory—its processes and contents—is fundamentally different in young childhood and infancy. This qualitative difference makes the formation and retention of memory from this time period in our lives difficult to assess. As we grow older, with time, practice, and brain development, our memories become more adultlike. Once into later adulthood, people refer to cognitive abilities in both negative and positive ways. You can be "over the hill" but also "older and wiser". Because memory involves so much nuance, both of these can be true! While there is an increased risk for dementia and Alzheimer's disease, and some skills do begin declining in young adulthood, we also maintain and grow our knowledge throughout our lives, even into later adulthood. Memory is complex, and there are many factors that can affect your memory throughout your lifespan.

4

EXTREMES OF MEMORY

Memory is often depicted in extremes in films and TV shows. Geniuses are often portrayed as ordinary people who have so-called photographic memory, allowing them to excel in their careers. Will in *Good Will Hunting*,[1] Lexi Grey in *Grey's Anatomy*,[2] Spencer Reid in *Criminal Minds*,[3] and Shawn Spencer in *Psych*[4] are all examples. At the other extreme, amnesia is a common trope in soap operas and movies. Often the result of head trauma, our character wakes up with no memory of who they are, and must spend the rest of the show solving mysteries about themselves.[5]

While extraordinary memory and amnesia are real phenomena, they do not occur in quite the same way or to the same extent as they are often shown in TV and film. Similarly, Memory Champions can remember a great deal, but the way in which many do this is probably different than most people think. In this chapter, we discuss exceptional memory and memory loss.

EXCEPTIONAL MEMORY

Wearing noise-canceling headphones to maintain concentration, a young man sits at a table and collects his thoughts. He opens his newly shuffled deck of cards and prepares his timer. He starts the timer and thumbs through the entire deck, memorizing the order of the cards as quickly as possible. He stops the timer and shuts his eyes.

DOI: 10.4324/9781003391166-4

A few minutes later, he is given an unshuffled deck and must put it in the same order as the deck he just memorized. This is the event Speed Cards that takes place at Memory Championships, and the man is Shijir-Erdene Bat-Enkh, who broke the world record. He memorized a deck of 52 cards in 12.74 seconds at the 2018 Korea OPEN Champs.[6] There are a growing number of national and international memory competitions, part of the growing popularity of mind sports, that take place every year. What does it take to achieve these incredible feats of memory? Are these mental athletes born with exceptional memory, or can anyone perform these triumphs with appropriate training?

These were the driving questions of the 2011 book *Moonwalking with Einstein* by Joshua Foer.[7] Foer, a journalist, interviewed memory champions to learn their secrets. He was surprised to learn that, no, none of the people he interviewed were savants or felt they had exceptional memory. In fact, they felt that *anyone* could learn to do these incredible memory feats with training and practice. Foer was skeptical but interested, and he volunteered to be the "anyone" and started training with the memory champions. The next year, he won the 2006 USA Memory Championship.

The mnemonic strategy that memory champions use has been used as far back as ancient Greece and Rome. This method of loci, sometimes called a memory palace, involves visualizing a familiar location and interacting with the to-be-remembered information in that location. For example, you might imagine walking through your home and interacting with items on your grocery list. Perhaps you envision walking through your front door and taking a sip of milk from a glass at the hall table, only to then slip on a banana peel. In general, the more interactive or bizarre the imagery, the better it is for your memory.[7] As an example in Foer's TED talk, he asks the audience to visualize a group of nude cyclists riding and then crashing into your front door, and Dorothy, Scarecrow, Tin Man, and the Cowardly Lion from *The Wizard of Oz* skipping out of your oven.[8]

While mnemonic strategies like the method of loci are incredibly effective, they do have some limitations. First, in order to achieve the kind of memory performance seen at the championship level, it does take quite a bit of deliberate practice (see Chapter 7). It also requires careful maintenance. Champions describe having to build and clean their memory palace. That is, once they have memorized one set of material in their location of choice (i.e., their memory palace) they have to clear it out in order to remember something else. Second, the usefulness of this technique is limited to the one-time memorization of serial-ordered information. The method of loci is great for remembering what items to purchase at the store or the order of a deck of cards, and less useful for understanding biochemistry or the difference between semantic and episodic memory.

It is possible to deliberately train and turn an average memory into one that can perform at championships, as shown by Foer. There are a handful of individuals who have truly exceptional recall of highly detailed information, and can do so seemingly without effort. Often, individuals with so-called photographic memory are depicted in TV and films as geniuses—people who are otherwise fairly normal but are able to be highly successful due to their gift of superior memory and intelligence. In Good Will Hunting, Will's girlfriend asks him how he is able to complete her organic chemistry homework despite having never taken a class in it.[1] She asks, "Do you have a photographic memory?"[1](01:20:13) She goes on, "You know, there are very smart people here at Harvard and even they have to study because this is really hard. And yet, you do it so easily, I don't understand. I don't understand how your mind works." Will explains, "Beethoven, ok? He looked at a piano and it just made sense to him. He could just play. . . . I couldn't paint you a picture, I probably can't hit the ball out of Fenway, and I can't play the piano. . . . When it came to stuff like that [academics] I could always just play." He is saying that he is normal in almost every way, but when it comes to memory and academic pursuits, he can just do it.

In truth, eidetic memory, the ability to remember information in near-perfect detail, what is often referred to as photographic memory, is incredibly rare. Further, reported cases of eidetic memory are more likely to occur in children than adults, suggesting that normal developmental changes disrupt this type of memory.[9] One possibility is that as we develop, we learn to generalize and build associations between concepts, and we lose some of our ability to identify and remember specifics. The ability to categorize and see relationships between things requires that we see them as less unique and individualistic. Every time we walk into a classroom, we do not have to learn that every chair is a chair that can be sat upon. We also do not have to remember each individual chair later to know what it does. Instead, we generalize; we learn what a chair is, and then they all just become chairs. As we learn that a bulldog is, in many ways, the same as a Great Dane, we may stop seeing and remembering as many of the unique differences between dogs.

The idea that exceptionally detailed memory comes at the cost of generalizations was explored in the short story *Funes the Memorious* by Jorge Luis Borges.[10] In the story, the titular character Funes acquired his heightened memory after being thrown from a horse and left paralyzed. While Funes seemed quite pleased with his superior memory, his acquaintance became somewhat exasperated with Funes as it was difficult to communicate without making generalizations. To most, one dog is still the same dog one minute to the next. To Funes, this seemed imprecise.

> He was, let us not forget, almost incapable of ideas of a general, Platonic sort. Not only was it difficult for him to comprehend that the generic symbol *dog* embraces so many unlike individuals of diverse size and form; it bothered him that the dog at three fourteen (seen from the side) should have the same name as the dog from three fifteen (seen from the front). His own face in the mirror, his own hands, surprised him every time he saw them.[10(p. 153)]

Every time Funes saw the dog, he wanted to call it something new. Every time he saw his hands, he was learning that they were his, as if they were something new. He could not generalize, and just call his hands, his hands.

Similarly, we can look at another form of exceptional memory, highly superior autobiographical memory (HSAM), a condition that leads individuals to have highly vivid and detailed episodic auto-biographical memories. People with HSAM do not use mnemonic devices like memory champions, nor do they perform better than others on tests of other types of memory, such as semantic tasks that require generating examples from specific categories (e.g., different types of vegetables or animals).[11] Rather, they have a highly supe-rior but specialized ability to remember even seemingly mundane events from their own lives in vivid detail. For example, they might vividly remember mundane events like the last time they took a train, or events that took place many years ago, such as the first time they drove a car. Jill Price, one of the rare individuals with HSAM, describes her memories "like scenes from home movies of every day of my life, constantly playing in my head, flashing forward and back-ward through the years relentlessly, taking me to any given moment, entirely of their own volition".[12(p. 2)] As more cases of HSAM are identified, researchers are able to better understand autobiographical memory and how to protect against the decline we see in normal aging and Alzheimer's disease[13] (discussed later in this chapter; see also Chapter 3).

Exceptional memory can also be seen in people with savant syn-drome. Savant syndrome is characterized by exceptional ability in a specific domain to a degree that is highly inconsistent with their overall level of functioning.[14] While savant syndrome can be found across all populations with neurological deficits, approximately 50% of those with savant syndrome also have autism spectrum disorder (ASD).[14] Memorization is the most highly reported exceptional abil-ity displayed by those with savant syndrome. Specifically, this type of superior memory appears to be automatic, unconscious, and highly detailed, but also weakly coherent. In other words, they are able to automatically remember an impressive amount of detail about a topic without much effort, but encounter challenges when asked to estab-lish meaningful connections between that information and a broader context. For example, they might be able to recall specific lines of dialogue from an actor's lengthy movie career but struggle to identify the main theme of their movies or role choices. A similar pattern is found in people with ASD, explaining why a substantial portion of those with savant syndrome are also diagnosed with ASD.[14]

Another form of exceptional memory can be seen in super recognizers, people who can recognize faces with extraordinary accuracy.[15] Our visual systems prioritize faces; we are particularly tuned to recognize that an object is a face. Even still, on average, people tend to be poor at matching unfamiliar faces, even when the two faces are presented simultaneously.[16] Super recognizers, however, are particularly good at remembering faces, even if they only saw the face briefly and a long time ago. For example, a super recognizer may be able to recognize a stranger out of context, like recognizing a person who used to work at a department store they visited years ago. These individuals are also particularly good at matching faces that are presented from different angles. Interestingly, on the other end of the spectrum are individuals who suffer from prosopagnosia, a perception disorder leaving a person unable to process faces holistically.[15] Because they cannot perceive faces the way people typically do, they are unable to identify people by their faces, even people very familiar to them, like a close family member or their own face.

While anyone can improve their memory with the use of mnemonic strategies like the method of loci, it seems that conditions like eidetic memory, HSAM, savant syndrome, and super recognizers are much more rare. Further, these conditions highlight the importance of forgetting in memory. Somewhat paradoxically, forgetting is related to the ability to remember *more* relational and associative information; we are able to take a broader, more integrated perspective.

MEMORY LOSS

While forgetting is a crucial part of memory, our ability to remember is functional, and too much forgetting can obviously be problematic. In TV or films, memory loss is often caused by a bump to the head and results in a loss of autobiographical information.[5] For example, in *The Bourne Identity* franchise, Jason Bourne wakes after being shot and nearly drowned and has no recollection of who he is.[17] While his autobiographical memory is gone, his procedural memory is not. He finds that he has a number of skills that one would expect of a secret agent. He is immediately embroiled in an international spy-thriller while trying to uncover his past. This is a somewhat sensational and inaccurate depiction of amnesia, though highly entertaining. (Matt Damon plays the title character in both *Good Will Hunting* and *The Bourne Identity*, making these two films an interesting memory movie double feature.)

Amnesia simply refers to memory loss. As such, there are a number of different kinds of amnesia. For example, we already discussed infantile amnesia in Chapter 3. Generally we can categorize amnesia based on the causes: post-traumatic amnesia, amnesia due to illness, dissociative amnesia, drug- or alcohol-related amnesia, etc. Regardless of the cause of amnesia, we can categorize the nature of the memory loss into two general categories: retrograde and anterograde amnesia. Retrograde amnesia is a loss of memory for events that happened prior to the damage or cause of amnesia and points to difficulties in accessing stored memories. (When retrieval impairments are implicated, like they are here, even saying memory "loss" can be a bit of a misnomer. Some ability is lost, possibly only temporarily, but the memories are not lost, per se. Rather, they just are not accessible. Imagine a library that is locked after hours. The books are not lost, they are just inaccessible after hours.) Anterograde amnesia is a loss of memory for events after the trauma or damage, and encoding, consolidation, storage, and retrieval have all been implicated in causing the deficits.[18] Further, amnesia can affect all different types of memory—declarative, nondeclarative, autobiographical, semantic, etc.

POST-TRAUMATIC AMNESIA

Post-traumatic amnesia occurs as the result of physical trauma to the brain such as concussions, car accidents, or even surgery. The extent and severity of the amnesia, whether retrograde or anterograde, generally corresponds to the extent and severity of the trauma. In the case of a mild concussion, someone may have trouble remembering the few minutes leading up to the head injury and the few minutes after the head injury. Severe or repeated concussions, however, can lead to much more extensive memory loss, impaired attention, slower processing speed, and reduced reading ability.[19]

One of the most extreme and complete cases of anterograde amnesia was the patient H.M., whose hippocampus was removed in an attempt to treat epilepsy. The hippocampus is a structure in the medial temporal lobe. (Medial means it is in the middle layer of the brain, and temporal means near the temple. If you were to put your finger to your temple and go in a few inches, that would be the medial temporal lobe. But definitely do not push your finger through your temple!) Thanks in part to the case of H.M., researchers now know that one of the major functions of the hippocampus is the consolidation of memories. Without a hippocampus, H.M. was able to hold a polite conversation—greet someone, ask how they are doing, remark on the weather, etc.—but would not remember anything after a few minutes. His working memory was intact, but he could no longer hold onto those memories over the long term. The surgery was done when he was in his 20s, and he lived into his 80s, making his loss of episodic and autobiographical memory particularly striking.

DISSOCIATIVE AMNESIA

Dissociative amnesia is memory loss resulting from a psychological cause rather than damage to the brain. As the name implies, the memory loss stems from a dissociation with either one's sense of self or experiences. For example, a dissociative fugue is the purposeful travel or wandering associated with forgetting one's own identity and other autobiographical information. But importantly, this impairment is often limited to episodic and autobiographical memory, and is often retrograde, meaning they forget personal details and events but can encode new ones.[20] Dissociative fugues are rare and typically occur after the experience of psychologically stressful events. For example, in one case study, an Ethiopian woman was found by her brother 14 months after she had left home. The incident that led to her disappearance was extremely stressful. She had been visiting a nearby village, and when she returned home, she found that her husband and three children had been slaughtered during an ethnic conflict. As a result of the conflict, she, along with many others, were moved to a displaced community camp. After several weeks in the camp, she began claiming that her husband and children had not died and became suspicious of her sister and her aunt. She was so upset that she was restrained. After 6 weeks in the camp, she escaped and could not be found. She was not seen by her family again until 14 months later when her brother unexpectedly found her in another town approximately 1,000 km from the displaced community camp.[20]

DRUG- OR ALCOHOL-RELATED AMNESIA

There are a number of different ways in which drugs and alcohol can result in memory loss. For example, amnesia is commonly induced as a part of general anesthesia during surgery so that patients do not remember the surgery. The drugs used to induce amnesia are most commonly benzodiazepines, a class of drugs that cause anterograde amnesia in high doses.[21] The drugs disrupt the encoding of information so that memories are never formed. The effect wears off as the drug wears off.

Long-term alcohol use or malnutrition can also result in memory loss. Korsakoff's syndrome involves both anterograde and retrograde amnesia of episodic memory and confabulation as the result of thiamine deficiency.[22] Confabulation refers to memories displaced in place or time or that never happened at all. For example, a patient might say that they went out to lunch with a relative yesterday when they have been hospitalized, or they might make up stories about working at a job they have never held. Patients with Korsakoff's are unaware of their confabulations, thus they are so-called honest lying.[23] Both long-term alcoholism and malnutrition lead to a deficiency in thiamine (vitamin B_1), which affects areas of the brain that are involved in memory.

While prolonged alcohol use can lead to memory loss, short-term alcohol use can also affect memory. Consuming large amounts of alcohol over a short period of time can cause anterograde amnesia, blocking the formation of new memories while intoxicated. These periods of blackouts are more likely to happen in people who have experienced blackouts before.[24]

DEMENTIA

Dementia is caused by a range of diseases or conditions that affect memory, thinking, and behavior, as well as the ability to perform everyday activities.[25] Dementia primarily affects older adults, but up to an estimated 10% of all cases start before age 65.

The most common causes of dementia are Alzheimer's disease, vascular dementia, dementia with Lewy bodies, and frontotemporal dementia.[25] In the case of Alzheimer's disease, neurons and connections between neurons (synapses) are lost, resulting in brain atrophy and cell death. Scientists are not exactly sure what causes loss of neuronal function in Alzheimer's disease, but it seems to be associated with plaques and tangles.[25] Amyloid plaques (buildup of the amyloid protein) and neurofibrillary tangles (collapsing of normally parallel strands of protein) disrupt normal neuron functioning, making it difficult for nutrients to pass through neurons and triggering inflammation in the brain. Vascular dementia is the result of cerebrovascular disease—difficulty with blood circulation in the brain, which results in brain damage. Similar to Alzheimer's disease, dementia with Lewy bodies is caused by a buildup of a protein in the brain. Frontotemporal dementia is caused by a number of different diseases that result in the degeneration of the frontal and temporal lobes. Again, these diseases involve the breakdown of normal protein functioning in the brain.

One of the challenges to diagnosing and treating dementia is that there are currently no definitive biomarkers of dementia-related brain damage.[25] In other words, so far you cannot get a blood test or tissue sample to see if you have dementia, although researchers are working on this.[26] Instead, by the time symptoms emerge and brain damage is visible through brain imaging techniques like fMRI (functional magnetic resonance imaging), the disease is already quite advanced. This makes it incredibly difficult to study the beginnings of dementia and to fully understand how best to prevent or treat dementia. Researchers' current understanding is that there is a genetic component to these diseases, but that certain environmental and behavioral factors can speed up or delay the progression of the diseases. Hypertension, diabetes, and smoking are all associated with an increased risk of Alzheimer's disease and other forms of dementia. Higher levels of educational and occupational attainment are associated with lowered risks of Alzheimer's disease and other forms of dementia.[25]

CONCLUSION: EXTREMES OF MEMORY—NOT AS SEEN ON TV

In the very first episode of *Criminal Minds*, Dr. Spencer Reid responds to the question "Are you a genius?" He says, "I don't believe that intelligence can be accurately quantified, but I do have an IQ of 187, an eidetic memory, and can read 20,000 words per minute. [pause] Yes, I'm a genius."[3(11:26)] In other episodes, Reid recites conversations verbatim from weeks prior and provides summaries of thousands of case files that he read in just a couple of hours. In reality, eidetic memory is extremely rare, even more so in adults. Hannibal Lecter has a memory palace, though it is not quite the same depiction as with memory champions.[27] In *50 First Dates*,[28] Lucy's memory resets every 24 hours, and she unknowingly lives the same day repeatedly. In reality, someone with anterograde amnesia would not recall events or conversations once they left working memory, a much shorter duration on the order of seconds or minutes. Memory, and, by extension, extremes of memory, is fascinating (we are biased, of course), and so it is not surprising to us that extreme memory abilities and deficits are so often part of the narrative in fiction. While rare, people can possess extreme memories—or train extreme memory performance—and the variety of memory abilities and deficits is diverse. Further, these extraordinary memories can help us better understand our own memories, which are extraordinary in their own ways.

5

MEMORY AND EMOTION

Humans can experience, and remember, a wide range of emotions. To show just how rich human emotions can be, consider a few unrelated examples:

A bride walks down the aisle and sees her partner, also wearing a white lacy dress, for the first time on their wedding day.

An elderly couple strolls through the city when a loud bang rings through the air, and large crowds of people start running and screaming.

A high school student finishes yet another weekly quiz and thinks they probably did well.

A teacher, preparing their new classroom for the upcoming school year, discovers a word they find offensive written in pencil on one of the desks.

A college student finishes their last final exam; this was their hardest class, but they know they absolutely aced it. They will be accepting their diploma next week but also saying goodbye to their college friends.

DOI: 10.4324/9781003391166-5

> Two women both discover they are pregnant. One calls their partner to celebrate the news, while the other dreads telling her ex.

From these examples, we can see positive and negative emotions. We can see varying strengths of emotion, from mild to quite strong. We can see the same event bringing mixed emotions for one person, and we can see the same event bringing very different emotions for two different people.

When we think about our own personal memories—episodic, autobiographical memories—we tend to remember some better than others. The memories we cherish, weddings, special birthdays, graduations, the birth of children, tend to be those that were created with great emotion. Traumatic experiences also come with strong emotions, and while we may wish we could forget these experiences, they sometimes feel unforgettable. In this chapter, we discuss whether our memories are enhanced for emotional information or events, and how trauma affects our memory.

AFFECT AND MEMORY

When we experience something emotional, like the scenarios at the beginning of this chapter, our affective, or emotional, response can be described across two dimensions, level of arousal and valence.[1] Level of arousal is our feelings of excitement and the physiological responses that accompany these (e.g., increased heart rate). Valence of our affective response indicates whether the emotions are positive and pleasurable or negative and unpleasurable.

When something evokes an arousing affective response, it is more likely that it will be remembered.[1] These benefits seem to be selective. Certain details may be remembered better about emotional experiences, but emotion does not lead to a picture-perfect memory. For example, in a medical emergency study described in Chapter 3, children 2–13 years old were asked about their memories of a serious injury and hospital treatment that occurred 5 years earlier.[2] The children's memory for the events were remarkably accurate given their age and the time delay, but memory for certain details was better than others. The children were better at remembering details that were central to their injury rather than peripheral details, and overall they were much better at remembering the injury than the details of the hospital visit. Another example is one that will be discussed in Chapter 8, weapon focus. The presence of a weapon when witnessing a crime often reduces memory for details of the perpetrator.[3] The presence of the weapon shifts focus from the perpetrator to the weapon, and this shift in attention affects memory. Higher arousal also changes the subjective quality of our memories. When we experience something in a high-arousal state, our memories for those experiences tend to feel more vivid than other experiences that do not cause arousal.

Emotional information seems to be prioritized during processing, such that we process emotional information automatically, leading to improved memory and increased vividness of the memory for that information.[1,4] For example, one experiment by Elizabeth Kensinger and Suzanne Corkin had participants study negative words that were either non-arousing (e.g., *sorrow, mourning*) or arousing (e.g., *slaughter, rape*).[4] Sometimes while they were studying the words they had a second task to do, during which they had to listen to different patterns of sounds and indicate when the pattern changed. This is called a divided attention manipulation because the participants must divide their attention between the two tasks—in this case, studying the words and responding to the sounds. Because our attentional resources are limited, performance on the tasks can be impaired, especially when the tasks are particularly difficult or require more attentional resources (see Chapter 6). When the participants were required to study the words in the divided attention manipulation, memory for the non-arousing words decreased, as we would expect. However, this did not happen for the arousing words. The effect on memory for the arousing words was very small, and memory for the arousing words was still vivid. Thus, when attention was divided, participants were still able to encode the emotional information almost as well as when their full attention was focused on studying the words. This supports the idea that emotional information is processed automatically and is prioritized.

The effects of emotion on memory get more complicated when examining the extent to which the valence affects memory for events. Some studies find that positive events are remembered better than negative ones, others find that negative events are remembered better than positive ones, and others still find that both positive and negative events are remembered to the same degree better than neutral events.[1] Because of this, it is unclear whether positive or negative events lead to superior memory. Some of this research suggests that negative emotional events are remembered more vividly, and with more detail, than positive emotional events, at least at first.

Part of the difficulty in studying the valence of emotional events is equating positive and negative events on as many variables as possible. If the positive and negative events differ on features other than just whether they are positive or negative, any differences in memory could be due to those other features, and not valence. A few researchers have addressed this issue by studying a single event that some people find highly positive and others find highly negative. For example, Elizabeth Kensinger and Daniel Schacter assessed memory for the final game of the 2004 Boston Red Sox and New York Yankees playoff series.[5] This series was considered highly emotional for fans because the teams are intense rivals. In addition, the outcome was extremely surprising. The Red Sox lost the first three games but were the first team in baseball history to come back from the deficit and win the series. Thus, Red Sox fans viewed the event as a highly positive emotional event, while Yankees fans viewed the event as a highly negative emotional event. They also surveyed baseball fans who were not fans of either team. The researchers surveyed fans about the details of the final game 6 days and approximately 6 months after that game. Overall, memory consistency for all participants was relatively low; even emotional memories are susceptible to forgetting and errors. However, the Red Sox and Yankees fans remembered more details than the other baseball fans. When comparing the positive and negative valence groups, the Yankees fans (negative emotions) had greater memory consistency across the 6 months after the game than the Red Sox fans (positive emotions). Red Sox fans (positive emotions) were more overconfident in their memory for the game than the Yankees fans (negative emotions).

The Kensinger and Schacter study, along with a few others, suggest negative emotional events are remembered better than positive emotional events. But again, the situation becomes more complicated when the time between the emotional event and when the person is asked to remember the event is extended. Carolyn Breslin and Martin Safer assessed the memories of Red Sox and Yankees fans for both the 2003 (the Yankees won) and 2004 (the Red Sox won) series games.[6] Importantly, they tested fans' memories 4–5 *years* after the games. Contrary to what Kensinger and Schacter found, Breslin and Safer found that after the longer delay, the fans had greater accuracy for the series that their favorite team won (positive valence). It is possible that memory for negative emotional events are more vivid at first but fade more quickly over time than memory for positive emotional events.[1] The goals of the rememberer can also influence how a memory is reconstructed, and may lead to differences in the way positive and negative memories tend to be retrieved. This also means that different people may remember emotional events differently, and the same person may remember emotional events differently depending on the context.[7]

Understanding how emotional events are remembered is a complicated issue. Overall, what is clear is that emotional events seem to be prioritized, remembered more vividly, and, often, remembered more accurately than events that are not emotional.[1,7] Of course, as has been discussed in this section, this does not mean that our memory for emotional information is perfect and infinite. Research has shown repeatedly that emotional memories are still susceptible to significant forgetting and distortion, even if they feel vivid and unforgettable.[1] In the next section, we discuss flashbulb memories, an area of research providing numerous examples of this.

FLASHBULB MEMORY

The term flashbulb memory is reserved for very specific types of memories that are emotionally charged and feel very vivid to the rememberer. Flashbulb memories are memories about the circumstances in which a person learns about a shocking public event that has personal meaning and consequences for the person forming the memory.[8] The thought is that the event for which the flashbulb memory was constructed is so emotional that the person is able to remember the event itself *and* the details surrounding how they learned about the event, the latter of which are a part of the flashbulb memory. Common examples include learning about the assassination of John F. Kennedy on November 22, 1963, the *Challenger* space shuttle explosion on January 28, 1986, Princess Diana's death on August 31, 1997, the 9/11 terrorist attack on September 11, 2001, the Brussels bombings on March 22, 2016, and the insurrection at the US Capitol on January 6, 2021. Of course, not everyone will have a flashbulb memory for the details surrounding the reception of each of these events. It is the events that have personal meaning for us that are most likely to form flashbulb memories. They are often described as so vivid and enduring that it seems like they will be remembered in detail forever. It is almost as though a flashbulb went off right at the moment when the person learned of the shocking event, and the circumstances at the time—the when, where, what was happening, and with whom—feel as though they are etched as a snapshot in one's mind.

The flashbulb memory is specifically for details surrounding how and when a person *learned* about the event, not the event itself. For example, we both have a shared flashbulb memory for the events at the US Capitol on January 6, 2021. We were both on a Zoom call with a third colleague, providing moral support to one another as we wrapped up events from the Fall 2020 semester and prepared for the start of the next semester at our respective institutions. All three of us were Zooming from our home offices. Althea saw something online, probably on Twitter, about the attack, and shared it. We were shocked, and wondered if an attack of that caliber really could be happening in Washington DC. We all started searching for information, but it seemed so outlandish that we were in disbelief. By the time we got off the call, the news was more concrete, and we all realized that a group of insurrectionists were attempting to prevent the peaceful transfer of power in the United States. I (Megan) remember feeling part uneasy and nervous, and part defeated and tired from the political turmoil over the last few years. These details, such as where we were, what we were doing, how and from whom we found out, and how we felt, are all part of our flashbulb memories.

Flashbulb memories are autobiographical in nature, and include the rememberer's experience learning about the public event. There can also be event details that are more semantic in nature. For example, we know that more than 2,000 people stormed the Capitol during the attack, and that Brian Sicknick, a Capitol police officer, died the following day due to injuries sustained during the attack. These are event details because they are specific to the event itself. The flashbulb memory is specific to the circumstances in which the rememberer learned of the event. For many people, the attacks on 9/11 provide another example. We, like so many others, have a detailed memory for where we were while watching the planes crash into the Twin Towers on the news. These personal details are a part of our flashbulb memories. We also know that four planes were a part of the attack, and this event detail is semantic.

A key aspect of the definition of a flashbulb memory is that the public event has personal meaning or consequences for the individual. Roger Brown and James Kulik reported that many more black Americans than white Americans had flashbulb memories learning that Martin Luther King Jr. had been assassinated.[8] As another example, many Swedes likely have flashbulb memories from when they learned of the 2017 Stockholm truck attack. However, likely far fewer in the United Kingdom or United States have flashbulb memories for this event. But I do. I (Megan) was traveling with my husband, and we were headed straight for the pedestrian street that was attacked, Drottninggatan. However, we were running behind that day, and so our train was one stop away when it stopped, and we learned of the attack. We had to get off the train and find a way to get back to our hotel without access to normal public transit, and with roadblocks. This event had personal significance to me because we were right there. I was in Sweden to give a talk, and upon returning, I told many of my colleagues what happened. Still, because the event did not hold large personal significance to them, they likely do not have flashbulb memories for this event even though I know I told them about it.

Flashbulb memories feel unique. They feel as though they are forever captured, and that we will never forget even the smallest details from the memory. However, memory researchers know that high confidence in a memory does not necessarily mean it is highly accurate.[9] Often it is difficult, if not impossible, to know the accuracy of one's own flashbulb memory. However, occasionally, when a large event occurs that is likely to produce widespread flashbulb memories, researchers are able to collect recollections from participants about their flashbulb memories somewhat immediately after the event took place, and sometime later. That is exactly what Ulric Neisser and Nicole Harsch did when the *Challenger* space shuttle exploded.[10] On the morning after the explosion, students wrote descriptions of how they heard the news, and answered a series of questions about the circumstances in which they learned about the explosion. Then, two and a half years later, they completed the same questionnaire, but this time they were also asked to indicate how confident they were in each detail of their memory from just guessing to absolutely certain. They were also interviewed over the phone.

The data are depicted in Figure 5.1. The researchers found that recollections were largely inaccurate when compared to the description provided the day after the event.[10] The memories were scored on a scale from 0–7, and many of the students (25%) had no consistencies across the two descriptions, scoring 0 points. Half of the students scored 2 points or lower. Only 7% accurately recalled everything 2.5 years later. Thus, the accuracy of the flashbulb memories were poor. Yet the students' confidence ratings tell a different story. The researchers calculated the average of the confidence ratings for each student. The students were, on average, largely overconfident in the accuracy of their memories. Approximately 30% of the students reported they were absolutely certain their memories were accurate, when in fact these students ranged from remembering everything accurately to remembering nothing accurately.

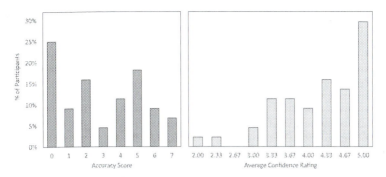

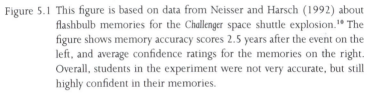

Figure 5.1 This figure is based on data from Neisser and Harsch (1992) about flashbulb memories for the *Challenger* space shuttle explosion.[10] The figure shows memory accuracy scores 2.5 years after the event on the left, and average confidence ratings for the memories on the right. Overall, students in the experiment were not very accurate, but still highly confident in their memories.

When the students were interviewed over the phone, they were presented with cues, based on their original report of how they learned about the *Challenger* explosion, to see whether these cues would lead to increased accuracy. The cues largely did not help and, in some cases, led to decreased accuracy.

The *Challenger* study is not the only one to report this pattern of results. In an impressive study, William Hirst and colleagues collected flashbulb memories of the 9/11 attacks, following up with the participants 10 years after the event.[11] They found that participants often provided detailed flashbulb memories over the 10-year period, but there were many inconsistencies in what they reported as their memory for learning of the event after the first year. Even still, their confidence in their memories remained high. After the first year, their (often inaccurate) recounts of how they learned about the 9/11 attacks largely did not change. In other words, the inconsistencies that became part of their flashbulb memories 1 year after the event continued to be reported for 9 more years.

It seems like emotionally significant events—events that are shocking and personally relevant, with vivid recollections—ought to be remembered as accurately as they feel to the rememberer. Emotionally charged events tend to be remembered better than neutral events, but that does not mean the memories are perfect. These memories can still contain errors and distortions, even when our confidence in them is near perfect.

TRAUMA, STRESSORS, AND MEMORY

Post-traumatic stress disorder (PTSD) is largely a disorder of memory, and is arguably one of the more severe impacts trauma can have on memory. In 1980, the American Psychiatric Association first recognized PTSD in their *Diagnostic and Statistical Manual of Mental Disorders* (DSM-III),[12] providing criteria for officially diagnosing an individual with PTSD. For a PTSD diagnosis, a person first experiences a trauma and then experiences a number of symptoms, including at least one symptom of reexperiencing the event (e.g., flashbacks, repeated memories or dreams). The most recent edition, DSM-V-TR,[13] defines trauma as requiring actual or threatened death, serious injury, or sexual violence. According to the DSM, a person with PTSD may be exposed to trauma through direct exposure, witnessing the trauma, learning the trauma happened to a close relative or friend, or indirect exposure to gruesome details as a part of one's job (e.g., first responders). Stressful events, even those that are highly stressful such as a divorce or custody disputes, would not qualify as traumatic under this definition.

There is some debate among clinicians as to what events count as traumatic, and the level of exposure necessary.[14] Clinical definitions of trauma are sometimes in stark contrast to the way the term is used more colloquially, or in the media. In the media, the term trauma has been applied to both a young star losing their luggage and a soldier witnessing horrific death during war.[15] Certainly these two are different; however, an experience and reaction to that experience does not need to qualify as clinical for it to affect a person, or their memory. Nontraumatic stressors could also affect memory. Thus, in this section of the chapter, we will review research on memory and both trauma and stress.

As I (Megan) am writing this, the most traumatic weekend of my life occurred 3 years ago, in June 2020. My memory for the events feels extremely vivid, unforgettable, and, in the beginning, even intrusive. (Trigger warning: pregnancy loss. To skip this story, skip the rest of this paragraph and the next paragraph.) My husband, Sam, and I started our Saturday morning like we had every other Saturday for the last few months: he made pancakes, and I read aloud from the pregnancy app on my phone. It was my first pregnancy, and I was 35 weeks along with our son, Spencer. After breakfast I cleaned. I had an unusual amount of energy that morning, and with only 5 weeks to go, I wanted to get things ready for Spencer's arrival. It was late morning when I finally sat down for a glass of water and grapes. After being seated for a while, I felt a panicked rush go through my body. Spencer was not kicking me, and this was a break in his pattern. I tried a few things, but still no movement. As we quickly left for the hospital, I remember worrying about how long a 35 weeker might have to stay in the NICU.

I can remember what happened next in more painstaking detail than can be included in this chapter. I remember I was wearing a blue and gray striped dress. It was an extremely hot day, and the sun was beating down as we parked and made our way to the hospital triage. I remember reminding Sam to put on his mask, and hoping that the hospital would allow him to stay. This was very early in the COVID-19 pandemic; I had only been in public for doctor's appointments, and Sam had not been permitted to join. I remember telling them everything had been fine the night before; I felt him at 11 pm before falling asleep. They asked me repeatedly if I had fallen (no). I remember the nurse struggled to find a heartbeat with the doppler, and then an attending physician brought the portable ultrasound machine. I remember holding my breath as she quietly moved the wand over my stomach. I remember the exact moment when I knew, and said, "You can't find the heartbeat, can you." I remember the sad look she gave me as she shook her head and said, "No." I could go on for pages and pages, describing every detail of my induction and delivering Spencer, stillborn, the following Sunday evening, Sam's first Father's Day. I feel as though I remember this weekend differently than I remember other events, even other major events in my life. From my own personal experience, these memories feel burned into my brain. I can see them in my mind, and I can feel them in my body, especially when it is a particularly hot and sunny day. Of course, my personal experiences are not necessarily universal, and our own introspections about our memories are not necessarily accurate. Just because some memories can be described in great detail, and feel very vivid, does not mean that they are perfectly—or even partially—accurate.

How trauma and memory interact has been a divisive issue, in the media and even among experts in the past.[16] Some have described, as I have, feeling like they could never forget their memories of traumatic events. Others have described pushing them out of consciousness until years later. Some therapists have reported that traumatic memories are often repressed to protect the person who experienced them, only to resurface years later, and possibly only after intensive therapy.[16] You may have also heard that experiencing trauma can impair one's memory abilities, leading to forgetfulness and brain fog.

Systematic research on trauma and memory increased dramatically starting around the mid-1990s, and the data quickly pointed to three conclusions, summarized succinctly by Richard McNally.[16] First, people remember traumatic experiences very well. Most who have experienced trauma can remember the experience, even too well. That some memories for trauma, and even chronic fear or negative symptoms, are remembered repeatedly and intrusively is called persistence.[17] This does not mean that all trauma is remembered in a way that is persistent. Sometimes people will make a concerted effort to avoid thinking about the traumatic experience, and avoidance symptoms is one of the required categories of symptoms for a PTSD diagnosis.[13] Some reviews have noted that attempts to suppress unwanted recollections are largely ineffective,[17] while others have pointed to studies where people do seem to successfully forget or avoid thinking about the trauma.[18] It is possible that in cases of persistence, environmental cues trigger the individual to remember the trauma. If they then try to push the memory out of mind by thinking of something else, that something else is now associated with the traumatic memory. Now a new retrieval cue has been created, and it becomes even more likely they will be cued to remember the trauma again in the future.[17, 18] Further, when memories are repeatedly brought to mind, this process strengthens the memory for those details (i.e., retrieval practice; see Chapter 6). Thus, persistent remembering can produce a vicious cycle.

Second, sometimes people who experience trauma do not think about the events, and this can go on even for long periods of time before remembering them again.[16] Third, just because a person who experienced trauma does not remember the events for some period of time does not mean they are unable to remember them (i.e., they do not necessarily suffer from amnesia—see Chapter 4—repression, or dissociation).

Persistent remembering can occur in situations less extreme than those categorized as trauma according to the DSM.[17] There is a lot of research investigating how stressors affect memory; however, the research on acute stress and memory, like that of emotion and memory, is rather complicated, with many seemingly contradictory patterns appearing across studies.[19] In a thorough review and meta-analysis examining over 6,000 participants, Grant Shields and colleagues found that whether acute stress enhanced, impaired, or had no effect on later memory was complex and depended on a number of factors.[19] The timing of the stressor—prior, during, or after encoding or retrieval—the relevance of the stressor to the to-be-remembered information, and even whether the remember was taking hormonal contraceptives all influenced later memory (when participants taking hormonal contraceptives were included, the effects of stress on memory tended to be smaller, pointing to the importance of sex hormones in the stress response and how this impacts memory processes).

CONCLUSION: EMOTIONAL MEMORIES, UNFORGETTABLE?

Emotional memories feel unforgettable. Unforgettable is not always ideal. It is important to remember that our memories are not like file cabinets; we do not file memories away in storage and then open the files when we want a detailed record of what happened. Memories, even emotional ones, are reconstructed at the time of retrieval. This means that errors can work their way into our memories, and our confidence does not always match the accuracy of our memories. It does seem that, at least some of the time, when a person experiences an arousing affective response, it plays a role in how the surrounding events are remembered. Much of the research suggests that some details from emotional events will be remembered better, but not always. We also know that repeatedly retrieving memories, even unintentionally, will actually strengthen them. In the case of trauma, we likely do not want those memories strengthened (but there are times when we do, the topic of Chapter 6). Whether we want to strengthen our memories or not, it is good to remember that we should not use the vividness of our memories as an indicator of their accuracy.

6

MEMORY AND EDUCATION

Imagine you have just learned that you will be tested on the contents of Chapter 2 in this book. What determines how well you perform on this test? Did your familiarity or prior experience with types of memory affect your understanding and subsequent memory? What about attention while reading? Does it matter how much time has passed between reading the chapter and taking the test? Finally, you might also be interested in how well you will remember the information beyond the test. While it may be advantageous to perform well on assessments, very often it is also desirable to remember information beyond taking a test, and to be able to use the information moving forward. Will you ever need—or be able—to remember and use this information after the test?

Whether you are a student, an educator, or a lifelong learner, research on memory and learning can provide valuable insights into how we can best learn, remember, and apply information. In this chapter, we discuss individual factors that affect how people take in information while they are learning it, strategies that can be used during learning that help people remember the information in the long run, the difficulty of taking what has been learned and applying it in different contexts (transfer), and how to increase the likelihood that transfer will happen successfully.

DOI: 10.4324/9781003391166-6

INDIVIDUAL FACTORS AFFECTING LEARNING
BACKGROUND KNOWLEDGE AND EXPERIENCE

Before you even step into a classroom (or any other learning situation), you come with a wealth of experience and knowledge that you have acquired up to that point. Your background knowledge and experience can have large impacts on your ability to learn new information.[1] When you have prior knowledge of the topic you are learning about, you not only have a stronger knowledge base to help you make sense of the new information,[2] you are probably more interested and engage with the material differently as a result.[3,4]

For example, imagine two university students starting their first computer science course. Both were star math students in high school and are eager to pursue a career in computer science. One student, we will call him John, has been programming as a hobby on his computer at home since middle school. The other student, we will call her Alva, has not. She used the computers at school and occasionally worked on her brother's computer but did not have one of her own. In class, Alva often feels a bit lost and struggles to keep up with the new terms and concepts. John, on the other hand, is already familiar with some of the concepts even if he does not know their exact name. While Alva is learning some of the basic terminology, John is asking insightful questions about applications—he knows from his prior experience how this information might be useful in solving a problem he has encountered in the past. In turn, John is more likely to feel energized by class discussions and is motivated to put in long hours studying. Alva, while initially determined and excited about a career in computer science, is more likely to feel discouraged and less excited about continuing her studies. John's background knowledge and experience have given him a huge advantage when learning about computer science.

This scenario, an all too familiar one in which men seem more likely to succeed in computer science than women, was explored in an episode of *Planet Money*.[5] Comparing data from the National Science Foundation, the American Bar Association, and the American

Association of Medical Colleges, the hosts reveal the percent of women in medical school, law school, the physical sciences, and computer science all steadily increased until 1984 when, notably, there was a sharp decline in the percent of women enrolled in computer science, and computer science only. The percent of women enrolled in all the other fields continued their steady increase upwards until the 2010s, while enrollment continued to decline in computer science.

What was different about computer science compared to the other science, technology, engineering, and math (STEM) fields? The hosts explain that in the late 1970s and early 1980s, home computers were marketed and sold almost exclusively to boys. This meant that by the mid-1980s, when women enrolled in university computer science classes, they had less experience with and background knowledge of computers relative to the men in their classes.[6] This gave men a leg up in computer science courses. Quickly, computer science was perceived as a "man's field". Women were much less likely to be interested in computer science as careers, and those who did enter computer science had more difficulty succeeding and were more likely to drop out than the men in their classes. It was not that women suddenly became less capable of doing computer science, but that a shift in the culture around computers made it difficult for them to attain the same level of background knowledge and experience as men. This example demonstrates just how important background knowledge and experiences are to learning something new.

ATTENTION

Another individual factor that can influence learning is your attention. Your ability to pay attention is influenced by your current physical state,[7, 8] emotions,[9] and experience with material.[10]

Generally, attention can be described in terms of focused attention and distributed attention. Focused attention is your ability to selectively attend to one task and ignore irrelevant information, whereas distributed attention is your ability to monitor different tasks and switch attention freely between them. For example, pretend you are reading a book in a crowded cafe while waiting to meet a friend. Imagine you become so engrossed that you do not notice the conversation at the table next to you. You also do not notice when your friend arrives, and you startle when they appear next to you. Your attention was *focused* on your book. When your attention is being used this way, you are able to engage deeply with the task in front of you at the expense of being aware of your surroundings. Focused attention is ideal for tasks that are complex or unfamiliar to you. (At least, so long as it is okay that you are far less aware of surroundings. Focused attention on complex and unfamiliar tasks is not ideal if ignoring your surroundings means you may be unsafe or miss something critical, like while driving.)

Now imagine that instead of reading your book, you have placed an order at the crowded cafe and are listening for your name to be called to retrieve the order. At the same time, you casually observe people at other tables, listen in on the conversation happening next to you, and notice as your friend walks in the door. Your attention is *distributed* among a few different tasks. When your attention is being used in this way, you are able to engage with multiple tasks at once; however, you are only able to shallowly attend to each one. Therefore, you are only able to engage in simple or very familiar tasks that do not require many attentional resources, like listening for your name and watching for your friend. If you were trying to read a book in the cafe while your attention was distributed—catching bits of the conversation next to you, listening for your name, and watching for your friend all while trying to read—you may not fully understand everything you read and would likely not get very far into the book. This is why it is often a good idea to limit distractions while trying to learn something new or study. If your attention is distributed due to distractions in your environment, you are less able to effectively engage with the primary task, learning.

When you learn new information, you typically rely on focused attention. You may have trouble focusing if you are tired, hungry, or dehydrated.[7, 8] It takes energy to stay focused! Your mood can also influence how well you can focus. Somewhat unsurprisingly, we tend to have better focus when we are in a happy and relaxed mood.[9] Several medical conditions can also lead to fatigue and brain fog, causing difficulties in focus.[11] In addition, several mental health conditions can affect attention (e.g., depression, anxiety, ADHD, etc.). While it is normal to have trouble focusing every now and then, if you find your inability to focus your attention is causing difficulties in everyday life, you may want to talk to your health-care provider or consult a mental health professional.

Your experience with the material you are learning can also affect your ability to focus. It is especially challenging to learn new things and engage in complex and unfamiliar tasks. These complex or unfamiliar tasks require more cognitive resources, so you may feel overwhelmed and unable to focus for as long as you would otherwise.[12] The more familiar and experienced you become with a task, the fewer cognitive resources that are required, and the easier it is to focus. One of the benefits of developing expertise in an area is that it takes less effort to do complex tasks (see Chapter 7). However, if a task is too familiar or simple, and you have an abundance of energy, you might find it boring and also have difficulty focusing.

Your ability to maintain focused attention is a complex relationship between the complexity of the task itself, your current physical and emotional state, and your background knowledge. Additionally, because focusing on a task takes energy and effort, it is normal to need breaks. The length of time you can maintain effective focused attention is highly variable; thus, how often breaks are needed depends on whether you are well rested, fed, hydrated, and in a good mood, as well as your experience with the task.

STRATEGIES TO IMPROVE LONG-TERM LEARNING

Often, when we are learning something new, our goal is to remember it for the long term. Certainly there are situations where the goal is short-term. For example, when I (Megan) was traveling in Sweden with my husband, we happened to get stuck just outside of central Stockholm during a terrorist attack, the 2017 Stockholm truck attack. We had to learn how to navigate back to our hotel without access to normal public transit, and with roadblocks. While this experience is one we will likely never forget (at least some details; see Chapter 5), we are unlikely to ever use anything we learned again (at least I hope not). But most of the time, when we learn something new, we hope to be able to remember it and use it in the future. Two of the most powerful strategies for long-term learning are retrieval practice and spacing.[13]

RETRIEVAL PRACTICE

Retrieval practice is the act of bringing information to mind from your memory.[13] By actively reconstructing the information based on the prompts to retrieve or clues that are available, you are improving your ability to do so again in the future. In this respect, retrieval practice works similar to the adage "practice makes perfect". For example, imagine you have started a new job and recognize a colleague you met recently. You typically get to work around the same time and see each other most days. If upon seeing him you say, "Hi, Jimmy!", it is more likely that you will be able to remember his name again in the future. However, this only works if you actively bring his name to mind. You could (and probably have) repeatedly recognized someone and simply said "hello!" without ever recalling their name. This leads to the somewhat awkward situation of having to ask for someone's name after having known them for a very long time. While you recognized them and said hello every day, you did not practice retrieval with their name.

There are many ways in which retrieval practice improves memory. Generally, we can categorize these into ways that retrieval practice directly improves memory—how retrieval practice in and of itself leads to better long-term retention—and ways that retrieval practice indirectly improves memory—how retrieval practice affects other things that improve memory.[14]

One of the reasons retrieval practice is so powerful is that it has a direct effect on long-term learning. We know from centuries of research that retrieving information decreases the likelihood that it will be forgotten over time.[13] For example, in a notable study, Henry Roediger and Jeffrey Karpicke examined how well university-student participants were able to remember a short passage after practicing retrieval compared to simply rereading the passage.[15] In the learning phase of the experiment, the students engaged with the information across four periods. During the first period, all students read the passage. Then, in one condition, participants reread the passage during the remaining three periods, so that they read the passage throughout all four periods in the learning phase (the Read Only condition). In another condition, participants reread during periods two and three, and then during period four they were instructed to write down everything they could remember about the passage (the Read and Retrieval condition). In the final condition, participants were instructed to write everything they could remember about the passage during all three periods after the initial reading (the Repeated Retrieval condition). Each period was 5 minutes long, so that all participants spent a total of 20 minutes with the passage. Next was the testing phase, to see how much the participants remembered about the passage. During the testing phase, participants were asked to write down as much as they could remember about the passage, and this took place after either 5 minutes or 1 week after the learning phase.

The data are depicted in Figure 6.1. Roediger and Karpicke found that after 5 minutes, memory of the passage followed a staircase function where participants in the Read Only condition recalled the most (83% of the passage), followed by participants in the Read and Retrieval condition (78%), and then participants in the Repeated Retrieval condition (71%).[15]

But wait, retrieval practice is supposed to *improve* memory! If we only looked at memory in the short term, retrieval practice would not seem very useful.[15] However, when we look at how much people remembered after 1 week, in the long term, we see the reverse effect.

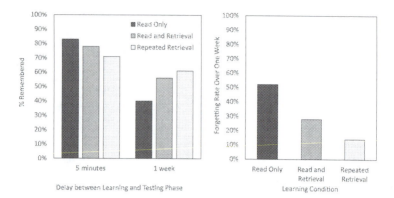

Figure 6.1 This figure is based on data from Roediger and Karpicke (2006) about the effects of retrieval practice on retention.[15] The figure shows the percent remembered by those in the three learning conditions after 5-minute and 1-week delays on the left, and the forgetting rates for each learning condition over 1 week on the right. Overall, repeated reading led to better immediate performance, but retrieval practice led to better long-term performance and less forgetting.

Participants who repeatedly read the passage across 4 periods (Read Only) recalled the least (40%), followed by participants who practiced retrieval in just 1 period (Read and Retrieval, 56%), followed by participants who practiced retrieval across 3 periods (Repeated Retrieval, 61%). We can calculate how much forgetting occurred over the week by calculating the difference in performance between the two testing delays, 1 week or 5 minutes, for each condition. This calculation shows that the Read Only forgetting rate was 52% of the passage in only one week! On the other end, the Repeated Retrieval forgetting rate was only 14% of the passage. Retrieval practice improves long-term memory by making it less likely that you will forget information over time.

In addition to direct effects, there are numerous indirect effects of retrieval practice on memory.[14] Practicing retrieval forces you to become more aware of how much you can and cannot retrieve. This helps you to identify gaps in knowledge, and can make future studying more effective and efficient (i.e., it can improve metacognition, discussed later in this chapter). Additionally, results from retrieval practice can provide valuable feedback to instructors about your progress.

There are many ways you can use retrieval practice as a learning strategy. Taking practice tests and quizzes is an obvious way to implement retrieval practice, but activities like group discussions, writing, drawing diagrams and maps from memory, and even casual conversations can all be ways to use retrieval practice as well. If you are trying to remember your coworker's name, retrieving it when you see him ("Hi, Jimmy") will help. As long as you are actively retrieving the correct information, you will improve your ability to remember it in the future.

SPACED PRACTICE

Another powerful way to improve memory is to space out your practice with that information.[13] Spaced practice refers to the advantage we get for remembering information that was spaced out over time, as opposed to massing all the practice together (i.e., cramming). For example, imagine you have set aside some time to learn or review material. It is a lot of information, so you decide that 3 hours is the amount of time you need for studying—maybe you even decided to dedicate some of that time to practicing retrieval. If you were going to mass practice together, you might block off 3 hours one evening to study (usually this occurs one or two nights before a test[16]). However, if you were to instead space your practice, you could study for 1 hour 3 evenings of the week, spread out over the week (e.g., Tuesday, Thursday, and Sunday). You spent the same amount of overall time—even engaged in the same learning strategies during your study session(s)—but because you spaced your practice, you are much more likely to remember the information later.

An experiment published by Katherine Rawson and Walter Kintsch highlights the spaced practice benefit.[17] In this experiment, participants studied a lengthy science text in one of three possible ways: reading it once (Read Once), reading it twice in a row (Massed), and reading it twice but with 1 week between readings (Spaced). Participants were then given a test over the material either immediately after they finished studying the material or 2 days later. When they were tested immediately, participants in the Massed condition remembered the most, and there was not much difference between the Read Once and the Spaced conditions.

But wait, spaced practice is supposed to *improve* memory! If we only looked at memory in the short term, spaced practice would not seem very useful.[17] When we look at the results from the test 2 days later, participants who spaced their reading remembered nearly twice as much as participants who were in either the Read Once or Massed conditions. Once again, we find that strategies that benefit long-term retention are not the same as strategies that are effective in the short term.

Spaced practice is really easy to implement. In research terms we call spaced practice a robust effect—it works under a wide range of circumstances with a wide range of materials.[13, 18] The key to using it effectively is to understand how long your working memory is. As long as you space out your practice by more than a few minutes, then you will get some benefit of having spaced your practice. Waiting long enough so that you get at least one night's sleep before studying again is even better. Of course, if you wait too long—on the order of several months or years—then you will have forgotten the information so much that spaced practice might not be as beneficial to your memory.

While it is possible to create tailored spaced practice schedules to optimize benefits,[19] practically it can be difficult to achieve the perfect spacing for optimal retention.[18] Because of this, our recommendation is to space practice as much as is possible, aiming to insert spaces of at least a couple of weeks between practice sessions.[19, 20] Generally, the more time that elapses between learning the material and needing to remember the material, the more time you have to space out your practice, and the longer the delays can be. If you have a test next week, you might want to space out your studying over a few days. If you have a test coming up next year, you can plan ahead so that you review across weeks or months. In the context of education, where students typically learn information over the span of several months, or a few years, there is a lot of flexibility for spaced practice, and consistent review spaced out over time is key.

There is one other important variable to consider with regard to spacing practice over time, and that is sleep. We know that quality sleep benefits memory.[7] That is, there are several different stages of sleep that we cycle through during a good night's sleep. Several of those stages have been shown to be important for improving memory.[21] So if you want an extra boost to long-term retention, then getting at least one night's sleep between spacing practice sessions will likely be more impactful than spacing within the same day.

ADDITIONAL STRATEGIES FOR LONG-TERM RETENTION

Retrieval and spaced practice are two of the strongest and simplest learning strategies to improve long-term retention but are far from the only strategies. Deans for Impact, a nonprofit in the United States, outlined several key cognitive principles that determine how students learn and retain new information based on research from cognitive psychology.[22] In addition to retrieval and spaced practice, they describe the importance of elaboration and interleaving. Elaboration focuses on asking how and why questions to create meaning. This provides a framework for understanding that helps to connect ideas. Interleaving involves mixing up practice of related, but different, types of content. Interleaving helps the learner compare and contrast information and distinguish between them. For example, if students are learning about mathematical operations like subtraction, addition, division, and multiplication, then it is more effective to interleave practice of the different problem types, than to block them (i.e., practice all the addition problems, then all of the multiplication problems, etc.).

While there are many more strategies that can improve memory, the strategies listed here are the ones that have the most evidence to suggest their effectiveness and are the most widely applicable. No matter who you are or what you are learning, you will be able to improve your long-term retention of information by using these strategies.

HOW CAN I TELL IF I WILL REMEMBER THIS LATER?

One challenge to using learning strategies is monitoring, or assessing, how well they are working, and then taking action based on these assessments. Do I already know this information well enough to stop studying, or do I need to keep studying? What strategy should I use, and when? Our ability to monitor our own learning, and the actions we take as a result, is what cognitive psychologists call metacognition.

Several factors influence our ability to monitor our learning. We can categorize metacognitive monitoring into experience-based judgments and theory-based judgments. Experience-based judgments are judgments we make about our learning in the moment based on how we feel. For example, we tend to judge something as easier to learn (and therefore more likely to be remembered in the long term) if it feels familiar or if it is easy to process. For instance, people will rate themselves as more likely to remember something in the future if it was written in a larger font compared to smaller font.[23] Objectively, we know that font size should not affect memory as long as it does not impede on your ability to read the material in the first place. However, in the moment it *feels* easier to read the words presented in bigger font. When making a judgment about how well we remember it in the future, we associate that ease of processing with knowing it better, and thus we (erroneously) think we will remember it better. Theory-based judgments, on the other hand, are judgments based on beliefs or theories that we hold about how our memory works. For example, we know that time affects learning. If we ask how much of this paragraph you think you will be able to remember 5 minutes, 5 days, and then 5 years from now, you will likely give decreasing estimates at each time interval. We understand and expect that we will remember less in 5 years than in 5 minutes. Interestingly, we only tend to use theory-based judgments when we are cued to use them.[24] So if we asked three different groups about their memory in 5 minutes, 5 weeks, or 5 years, on average their estimates would be about the same. Without having another time point to compare against, they are not cued to use their theory of how time affects memory when making that judgment. It is only when each person is faced with making a judgment for all three time intervals at once that they think about how time is related to memory, and they decrease judgments for the longer time intervals.

The second aspect of metacognition is the actions we take as a result of our monitoring, called metacognitive control. Once you have determined you will remember a lot or a little, what action do you take as a result? We hope that our discussion of effective learning strategies throughout this chapter provide some guidance for what to do next!

How well you are able to use metacognitive monitoring and control can also be influenced by your attitudes and motivations surrounding learning. Generally, we can think of monitoring, control, attitudes, and motivation as interacting in a cyclical process.[25] Deciding to actively monitor your learning requires motivation and knowledge. Continuing to do so after falling short of learning goals certainly requires a healthy and positive attitude toward learning. Thus how we learn depends on our background knowledge, attention, learning strategies, metacognitive monitoring and control, and attitudes and motivation.

APPLYING WHAT HAS BEEN LEARNED

One of the foremost challenges in education is the transfer of knowledge. Transfer refers to the ability to use information in a new or different context.[14, 26] For example, when I (Althea) taught psychology students how to write papers in psychology, I found that I needed to review many of the concepts they were taught in their English composition courses. Namely, how to structure an effective introduction, body, and conclusion. When I asked if these concepts were familiar, most students said that they were, but it did not occur to them to write a psychology paper in the same way as their English papers. They thought writing papers in psychology would be completely different than in English. They did not understand what transferred from one context to the next. In the past, our students have sometimes struggled to transfer what they have learned in one research methods class to a more advanced research methods class, when it is more obvious that past information can be applied. Transfer can be difficult, even when the two situations are relatively similar (like two psychology research methods courses).

Successful transfer requires learners to recognize that there is a similarity to already-learned information, recall the already-learned information, and then link the already-learned information appropriately in the new situation.[26] An error in any of these three steps—like lack of recognition that the two are similar, inability to remember aspects of the already-learned information, or inability to see which features of the already-learned information link to the new context—can inhibit successful transfer. In biology, for example, students may learn about how acidity plays a role in human digestion in one course, and then about ocean acidification in another.[26] If they recognize that the two topics are related, can recall what they learned about acidity in human digestion, and appropriately apply the underlying principles from acidity in human digestion to ocean acidification, they have transferred their knowledge.

Successful transfer is more likely when we have well-developed schemas. Having an organized framework to draw upon makes it easier to see similarities and make links from already-learned information to the new situation.[26] In the acidification example earlier, after working with the examples of human digestion and ocean acidification, students may develop a schema for how acidity affects biological organisms in general. That schema would make it easier to transfer their knowledge about acidity to many other situations—like soil acidification or food safety. Generally, the more experience we have in an area, the better developed our schemas are (see Chapter 7).

CONCLUSION: UNDERSTANDING MEMORY CAN IMPROVE YOUR LEARNING

Research on memory has a lot to say about the best—most effective and efficient—ways to learn and remember information. In education, the focus is often on higher-order learning and application. Can a student take information from class and use it in a unique way? Can they use it in their careers, or the real world? Memory is critical here, because you cannot apply what you do not know. Setting up an environment that encourages focused attention and engaging in spaced practice and retrieval practice to reinforce learning and slow forgetting all serve to help increase our memory and our deeper understanding of material. Reinforcing learning allows us to build critical background knowledge such that when we attempt to learn something new, our prior learning supports our endeavors. Once we have developed a strong understanding, then, and only then, can we transfer what has been learned to a new context.

7

MEMORY AND EXPERTISE

As experts in human memory, we both have a distinct advantage when we read and learn about new research in memory compared to someone who does not have as much experience with memory research, like our students. We are both faster to evaluate and remember research related to memory, as well as more patient when pouring over manuscripts about memory compared to our students. We remember the names and dates of important papers in our field and are quick to supply answers to very specific questions about memory. While this skill may seem impressive in this very limited context, our expertise does not necessarily extend to other areas. For example, I (Althea) love making spreadsheets and comparing research data on human memory and learning. I enjoy thinking critically, digging into details, and making comparisons. I can spend hours a day reading about expertise development and memory in order to determine how I should teach skills in my classes. However, when making larger purchases, I hate reading product reviews and get easily overwhelmed by the details. I will throw my hands up in frustration after 10 minutes of comparing laptop specs. Within my area of expertise, I am clearly quite capable of thinking through complex information and using data to inform my decision-making—but struggle outside of my area of expertise.

Experts—people who have a wealth of knowledge and experience in a domain—not only remember more about their area of expertise

DOI: 10.4324/9781003391166-7

but also process new information more quickly in their area. In this chapter, we discuss how expertise changes memory, how to develop expertise, and benefits and drawbacks of expertise.

HOW EXPERTISE SHAPES MEMORY

Compared to novices, experts have a wealth of knowledge to draw upon for making decisions. Experts do not just know more about a topic, the way they organize and use their knowledge is different from a novice as well. Experts organize their knowledge by meaning, forming a wealth of associations among their knowledge base, and use that knowledge in a way that allows them to expand their working memory.[1-4] Here is a very simple example. If we present a series of 22 letters to you, it would likely be difficult for you to remember those letters in perfect order if they are random. However, if you are reading this book, then you have some expertise in reading the English language. If we present a series of 22 letters that you can group together into meaningful words, like P-S-Y-C-H-O-L-O-G-Y-O-F-E-V-E-R-Y-T-H-I-N-G, then you will be much better able to remember them all in perfect order. In a way, you are expanding your working memory; you do not have to remember each individual letter but rather connect the letters together to form a concept, the title of this book series, and just remember that one thing.

A classic study with chess experts demonstrates clearly that experts organize their knowledge differently—that they have rich and detailed schemas in their area of expertise. William Chase and Herbert Simon asked chess experts and chess novices to remember the location of chess pieces on a board.[1] Unsurprisingly, the chess experts were better at remembering the location of pieces. However, they were only better when the pieces were arranged in a way that followed the rules of the game. If the pieces were arranged randomly, then there was not a significant difference between experts and novices (in fact, the novices performed slightly better than the experts!).[1] Experts were able to glance at a chess board and make sense of how pieces were arranged, if the board followed the game rules. Their expertise allowed them to group items together in meaningful ways that helped them to remember the board later. They did not just see individual pieces on the board—they saw an effective opening strategy or a risky middle game gambit. Since these board positions had meaning to the expert players, they were able to use that to help them reconstruct the memory of the board pieces later. But when the pieces were arranged randomly, with no meaningful relationship to game mechanics? Their expertise was not useful in that context.

However, you do not have to be an expert to develop and use schemas, at least not in the technical sense. Any time your prior experiences help you to understand the rules of a scenario so you can make sense of it, you are using a schema. Take the example from Chapter 2 about going to a new restaurant. You likely have a schema of what to expect when you go to a restaurant based on your past experiences, and you can use your restaurant schema to visit new restaurants. We visited England and went out to dinner with some colleagues. Most of the dinner party were Americans, like us, and we remarked on how slow the service was. Our colleague from the United Kingdom was confused by our remark and asked us what we meant. We told her we were surprised that no one had come over to refill our waters or to take our orders. She kindly explained to us that it was considered rude to interrupt diners in conversation, and that servers were waiting around the room for us to signal to them that we were ready. To our American (and polite Midwestern) sensibilities, it seemed a bit rude to wave a server to the table, and it took some getting used to. For us, waving a server over signals that we are unhappy and demanding attention immediately. This experience did not match our schemas for how ordering at a restaurant usually works. It seems a bit strange to label us as expert US-restaurant-goers (although Megan does have a bit of experience as a hired "undercover" reviewer and critic for a restaurant group), but certainly we had a wealth of experiences to draw upon that led us to develop a specific schema for how to interact with waitstaff. Now, after a few experiences eating at restaurants in the United Kingdom, we have greater expertise than we did before. Our schemas are now more detailed and include US and UK restaurant customs.

Similarly, most adults have a schema for how to procure groceries in their local area. However, when the COVID-19 pandemic hit, shutting down many services and changing the social rules, our schemas were changed rapidly. Getting groceries took a great deal of adjustment and more working memory power! Now in some areas, we had the added tasks of remembering to put a mask on before entering the store, remembering to go the correct way down one-way grocery store aisles, remembering not to touch our faces, staying further away from other people, wiping things down or even being asked to put on gloves prior to touching produce in some areas, and avoiding certain shopping times that were dedicated to seniors and those with compromised immune systems. What used to be a very easy and routine task—going to the grocery store—became much more challenging. Previously we could rely on well-developed schemas to reduce demands on working memory. But when the schema changed, we were no longer experts, and the task became much more challenging, requiring more conscious thought and working memory capacity. Over time, and repeated experiences, we developed our pandemic shopping expertise as we acclimated to the new social rules, and the task became easier again.

Another way in which the organization of memory is different in experts than in novices is in associations. Experts organize their knowledge by meaning, heavily cross-referencing each piece of knowledge so that on the whole their knowledge is more highly associated.[4] For example, novice physicians' knowledge of diseases is based on the most common features of the disease. Their knowledge does not yet have as many shared features of, or connections to, other diseases, compared to expert physicians. Expert physicians, on the other hand, appear to heavily cross-reference information about diseases, resulting in rich networks of associations among diseases with similar symptoms.[5] Not only do expert physicians see more connections among diseases when trying to make a diagnosis, they also have a tendency to consider more options when making a diagnosis.[6] Their expertise gives them both more associations, and the persistence to sift through more options, leading to better diagnoses. Similarly, connoisseurs of music, literature, or cuisine have more nuanced and cross-referenced networks of information about their areas of interest. A metalhead is able to classify bands into complex networks of sub-genres, noting similarities with similar sub-genres (i.e., heavy metal, black metal, nu metal, Viking metal, etc.). Avid fans of genre literature create lists of recommendations based on particular tropes, themes, and narrative techniques on social media. TikTok, Instagram, and YouTube all have thriving book communities (booktok, bookstagram, booktube) where reviewers recommend books based on tropes, themes, and narrative techniques. Looking for a boy next door, fake dating, enemies-to-lovers romance? A fantasy heist with a novel magical system? A postapocalyptic sci-fi written by a woman? You can find no end of recommendations from experts with rich connections across literature in their area.

In addition to simply remembering more information in their areas of expertise, experts are also better at using that information. For example, expert calculators in Japan who learned how to do calculations using an abacus are eventually able to do the calculations without a physical abacus.[2] These expert abacus users are able to use visual imagery to imagine the abacus and perform long calculations. Their long-term knowledge and experience with abacus calculations allows them to essentially expand their working memory when using (or imagining using) an abacus. Experts are able to hold more information in mind while completing complex tasks because they can rely on the rich associations, schemas, and procedural memories they have in their area of expertise to help them.[3] But only in their area of expertise. The expert abacus calculators in Japan can only leverage their abacus expertise when performing calculations. Any boost they get to working memory is specific to their area of expertise and does not transfer to other unrelated situations where they might use working memory.

DEVELOPMENT OF EXPERTISE

Experts can be impressive and awe-inspiring when they are highly skilled or display their vast knowledge. People pay a lot of money to see professional athletes and musicians use their skills. Similarly, we tend to be impressed by people who hold highly skilled jobs like lawyers, doctors, and engineers. It may be tempting to think that these people were just born with a natural talent that led them to their career, but research on expertise highlights the importance of practice in achieving this high level of skill.[7]

You may have heard of the 10,000 hour rule, a concept that became popular after Malcolm Gladwell's best-selling book *Outliers*.[8] According to his interpretation, it takes roughly 10,000 hours to become an expert in something. While this certainly highlights the immense amount of practice it takes to achieve expertise, thinking an expert needs 10,000 hours leaves out some of the important nuances. This rule is based on research done by Anders Ericsson and colleagues.[9] They interviewed promising young violinists and pianists at a German academy and compared the daily routines of these expert musicians with novices. Based on detailed interviews, they calculated that the experts had accumulated roughly 10,000 hours of practice on their instrument by their early 20s, compared to the novices who had accumulated only 2,000 hours.

The amount of practice the musicians acquired was impressive, but the way they were practicing was what the researchers found most interesting. Their practice was *deliberate*. Deliberate practice is purposeful and self-directed practice where learners gain feedback on their performance.[10] There are several key aspects to this type of practice. First, as the name implies, this is practice that is done deliberately on the part of the learner. In other words, being forced by someone else to practice is not as effective. The practice should be self-motivated and goal-oriented. This first step—being self-motivated—is somewhat difficult for beginners,[11] perhaps because they lack the experience necessary to monitor and correct their own performance.

Tied to this ability to be self-motivated is the opportunity for immediate feedback. Feedback allows learners to improve their understanding of their particular knowledge or skill set and to adjust their performance accordingly.[9] Initially, this feedback needs to come from other experts—teachers, coaches, trainers, etc.—but as you gain experience, you are better able to monitor your own performance. When beginners make mistakes, they may not realize that they have made a mistake, let alone what steps they can do to correct it. Experts, on the other hand, are able to monitor their performance more accurately and not only make small adjustments but see the improvement from those adjustments. Thus, it is easier for experts to see the benefits of their deliberate practice and remain motivated.

Finally, deliberate practice does involve repetition, the element of gaining expertise that seems to be the focus of the 10,000 hour rule. Importantly, when done with self-motivation and opportunities for feedback, repetitions allow learners to make small, incremental adjustments.[9] Small adjustments and feedback combine to make this an iterative process—each attempt can improve upon the previous. If a minor adjustment did not work the way you had hoped, you can try something else in the next repetition, noting how it compared to the previous attempts.

There are several constraints to engaging in deliberate practice.[9] Time is perhaps the most obvious. Deliberate practice requires repetition and feedback, which require dedicated portions of time to achieve. The professional musicians Ericsson and colleagues interviewed were spending 10–20 hours a week practicing by the time they were 13 or 14 years old, and 30 hours per week practicing by the time they were 20 years old.[9] Outside of the sheer amount of time it takes to engage in deliberate practice, there are other barriers like opportunity and access. Teachers, trainers, and coaches often cost money, and even if you can afford them, you may not have access to them. Further, just setting aside the time to engage in deliberate practice may take away from time that could be spent earning a wage. Finally, the initial challenges in motivation may present a significant barrier to practice.[11]

Another challenge to engaging in deliberate practice may be due to the type of expertise one is trying to gain. For example, one of the challenges in medical education is obtaining feedback after making medical diagnoses.[12] There is usually some time between diagnosis, treatment, and feedback from the patient regarding whether the treatment is working. This problem is only exacerbated when dealing with rare conditions and diseases, simply because physicians do not get as much practice with these cases. A similar problem arises in surgery. Surgeries are relatively high-stakes procedures, requiring surgeons to have a high level of skill with a procedure before performing it on a patient. Thus, there is a high degree of interest in the medical community in training methods like virtual reality and surgical simulations,[12] where surgeons can engage in the high number of repetitions needed to develop their skills without putting actual patients at risk.

BENEFITS OF EXPERTISE

Having expertise in an area leads to several benefits when dealing with information in that area. As noted earlier, one obvious advantage is a benefit to memory for the content within the area of expertise. Expert chess players are able to glance at a chess board and very quickly memorize the positions of chess pieces on the board.[1] The chess board makes sense to them and holds meaning in a way that eludes novices. Another benefit described earlier is the boost experts can gain when using working memory in their area of expertise. Expert abacus users can simply imagine the abacus to assist them with calculation, temporarily expanding their visual working memory.[2, 3]

Another benefit of expertise is in problem solving. Because experts organize their memory based on meaning, with rich associative networks,[4] they are better able to solve problems that rely on that meaning. For example, when asked to categorize physics problems, novices categorize problems based on surface features (i.e., whether an incline was involved or whether a spring appeared in the problem), while experts categorize problems based on physics principles.[13] Experts are better able to solve problems in their area of expertise, thanks, in part, to how their memory is organized.

Finally, once established, expertise confers a rich-get-richer type of effect where it is easier for experts to learn new information in their area of expertise. Simply having prior knowledge of a topic helps you to learn more about that topic.[14] As described earlier, expertise involves a large motivational component in addition to all of the memorial benefits already discussed. Experts are more likely to be interested in and reengage with material in their area of expertise. Higher prior knowledge of a domain can also lead to increased motivation, and possibly more accurate metacognitive monitoring (see Chapter 6), to learn new information.[14]

DRAWBACKS OF EXPERTISE

While there are obvious benefits to expertise, there are also drawbacks. While generally advantageous, the way in which memory is organized in experts is also very specific to their area of expertise. Expertise is specialized. As experts in cognitive psychology, we both tend to think about learning as cognitive psychologists. This means we do not necessarily think like social psychologists, musicians, or administrators about learning. When experts approach problem solving, they are susceptible to Einstellung (attitude) or mental set.[15] Experts tend to view problems in a certain way, which can prevent them from seeing different, creative solutions. Earlier in the chapter, we mentioned that chess experts were only better at remembering chess pieces when they were arranged in a way that followed the game rules. When the pieces were randomly placed on the board, novices slightly outperform experts.[1] There are actually many documented instances where novices seem to outperform experts. Baseball novices remembered more non-baseball information from a text describing a game than experts.[16] Practicing doctors, while better at diagnosing patients, remembered fewer case-specific details than medical students.[17, 18] Expert accountants are less likely to apply new tax laws than novices.[19] And expert bridge players have a harder time adapting to a new version of the game that changes the bidding procedure.[20]

Similarly, another disadvantage that experts have is the inability to see things as a novice would. They forget how challenging or difficult a task might be because it comes easily to them.[21] This is often called the curse of knowledge. While experts clearly have advanced knowledge and a wealth of experience in an area, the curse of knowledge can make it difficult for them to teach their skill set to others.

CONCLUSION: ANYONE CAN BECOME AN EXPERT

Expertise shapes memory in a number of ways. Experts not only remember more about their area of expertise, their memory is organized according to meaning and has a wealth of associations that helps experts use their memory more effectively. Expertise is developed through deliberate practice—an iterative process that involves repetition, feedback, metacognitive monitoring, and motivation. Once developed, expertise helps you remember more, use more information with long-term working memory, solve problems, and helps you to learn more too! Often, people think that talent and skill are natural abilities—something you are either born with or you are not. While genetics plays a role in expertise development (as a short woman, Megan was never going to be a star American football or basketball player), it is far from the only factor. This is true of intelligence, as discussed in the *Psychology of Intelligence* volume in this series,[22] and other areas. We are memory experts, and this took many years and hours of deliberate practice, but we also work to increase our expertise in other areas (e.g., crocheting, TTRPGs, wine tasting—that one is both of us). We can become experts by engaging in deliberate practice, and so can you!

8

MEMORY AND THE LAW

In Serial[1] season one, a podcast that saw over 300 million season one downloads[2] and led to explosive interest in shows about true crime, Sarah Koenig tells the story of Hae Min Lee's death in 1999, and her ex-boyfriend Adnan Syed's conviction for her murder. (Since then, there has been a lot of legal back-and-forth, likely because of Serial. As of 2023, Syed's conviction may be overturned.) Koenig explains that before working on the story, she never really thought about how hard it is to account for time in a detailed way. As a demonstration at the beginning of episode one, she asks her 18-year-old nephew and some of his friends to try to recall what they were doing 6 weeks back. Her nephew, Sam, says he is pretty sure he was in school, and then actually he thinks he worked that day. Sam's friend sounds more confident in his answers initially, and says he went to the movies that night with Sam. When Koenig reveals Sam already reported he was at work, the friend says, "Oh, then it wasn't that night then."

Whether you were at work or at the movies 6 weeks ago might not matter much in most situations. Most of us would struggle to give a detailed account of exactly what we were doing 6 weeks ago. Unless there is some special reason for you to remember what was going on—it was your birthday, you had a big deadline at work, you committed a crime that you do not normally commit—then it can be particularly difficult to accurately piece together details from that day. And yet, if you find yourself involved with the legal system, you

DOI: 10.4324/9781003391166-8

may be asked to remember details like this, and the stakes can be extremely high. In criminal investigations, an eyewitness' ability to accurately remember details, and their confidence in their recollections, can be the difference between incarceration and freedom, or even life and death. In this chapter, we discuss factors that can affect the confidence and accuracy of eyewitness memory.

CONFIDENCE IN MEMORIES

Sam and his friend highlight two things about remembering. First, that it can be difficult to remember even larger details from a particular time and place with certainty. Second, our confidence in our recollections is not a perfect gauge of our accuracy.

Take the case of Jennifer Thompson and Ron Cotton as another example. In 1984, Ron Cotton was arrested for the rape of Jennifer Thompson.[3] He was identified by Thompson in a photo lineup as the man who raped her. When the police questioned him, he provided a detailed account of where he was and what he was doing. However, he got his weekends confused, giving the police reason to think he was lying. He was arrested and put in a physical lineup, and Thompson again picked him from the lineup. Thompson was sure she had picked the correct man; during the attack, she studied her rapist so that she would be able to identify him later. She testified in court, and Cotton was convicted and sent to prison for life and 50 years. In 1987, Cotton was granted a new trial. During this trial, Cotton's defense attorney presented an alternate suspect for the crime, Bobby Poole, who was also in prison for rape. Poole also had bragged about raping Thompson. With both Poole and Cotton in the courtroom, Thompson still identified Cotton with extreme confidence. Cotton was convicted again. However, in 1995, DNA evidence cleared Cotton of all charges and showed that the rapist was Poole. Cotton spent over 10 years in prison for a crime he never committed.

One of the more shocking details of this case, at least to us and our students when we teach about it, is that Thompson did not recognize Poole, the real rapist, during Cotton's second trial. Thompson has stated that she has gone back to that moment in her mind many times, and she just simply did not recognize Poole.[3] She was absolutely certain she recognized Cotton as her attacker. This case is not an isolated incident—legal systems are filled with cases that have been overturned as a result of DNA evidence, and, at least within the United States, the vast majority of the exonerated individuals were mistakenly identified by an eyewitness.[4]

How can an eyewitness be so confidently wrong on the stand? We know from cognitive psychology research that confidence is not perfectly correlated with accuracy.[5] In other words, just because an eyewitness says they are absolutely certain does not mean that they are also absolutely accurate. In addition, by the time an eyewitness is testifying in court about their memory of a crime, a great deal of time has passed since the actual event, and the witness has typically revisited this memory multiple times through identifications, questioning by law enforcement, and pretrial meetings. By this point in the book, you are quite familiar with the issue at hand: accessing our memories is not a benign event. Our ability to remember events, recognize faces, and reliably recall mundane, or even important, details of our lives is more fragile than most think. Our memories are not like tape recorders or file cabinets. Instead, our memories change every time we access those memories. Memory is reconstructive; when we are given a retrieval cue, like a prompt to remember a specific date and time, we use that cue to piece together what we think happened, and outside influences can bias the memory, and our confidence in the memory.

Eyewitnesses who are extremely confident on the stand but turn out to be wrong do not necessarily start out that confident. Both from real cases of mistaken eyewitness identification and experimental data, we know that when a mistaken identification in a lineup is made, it is often done slowly and with low confidence.[4] The problem is that if the eyewitness mistakenly identifies the suspect, then the eyewitness often receives confirmatory feedback. Think of how a typical lineup is conducted. An eyewitness is presented with an array of options, either of people who are physically present or, more often, photographs of individuals. Among the options, there is a single suspect who, importantly, may or may not be the actual culprit. There are also a number of fillers who are known by law enforcement to be innocent but are similar in appearance to the suspect. If the eyewitness picks one of the fillers in the lineup, no charges will be filed against the innocent filler. However, if the eyewitness does pick out the suspect, then any feedback will be confirmatory, suggesting the eyewitness selected correctly. Confirmatory feedback after an identification increases an eyewitness' confidence in their memories but, of course, does not increase the accuracy of their identification.

In the original experiments examining confirmatory feedback,[4,6] participants viewed a simulated crime and then were given a photo lineup and asked to identify the culprit. However, the lineup intentionally did not include the culprit, inducing high rates of misidentification. After the lineup, some of the participants were told "good you identified the suspect". The participants then answered a number of questions about their memories, including how certain they were when they made their identification and how well they could see the culprit in the video. When participants were given confirmatory feedback in their misidentification, they were much more likely to report that they had a great view and they were certain they were correct during identification. The confirmatory feedback increased their overall confidence in their memory, explaining how a witness might make an identification with low confidence but state they are absolutely certain when they testify in court. Further, this feedback has a cumulative effect on memory, making memory distortions larger and larger over time. Take the Thompson-Cotton case as an example. Thompson's initial identifications were slow; her recognition of Cotton was not immediate.[3] After the physical lineup, she was told that she picked Cotton both times. Presumably she received more "doses" of confirmatory feedback in future meetings with law enforcement prior to Cotton's first trial. By the time she was faced with her real rapist during Cotton's second trial, she was so confident in her memory of Cotton raping her that she did not even recognize the real rapist!

Confirmatory feedback, like "good you identified the suspect" inflates incorrect eyewitness' confidence such that by the time eyewitnesses are testifying, confidence in one's memory does not signify accuracy. However, in spite of this, confidence in a person's memory is often used as a proxy for the accuracy of that memory within the legal system, at least in the United States. For example, the *Neil v. Biggers* (1972) US Supreme court case ruled that highly confident eyewitness identifications are likely to be accurate.[7] We now know from psychological science that this simply is not true! Yet even in the twenty-first century, confidence and accuracy are assumed to be tightly linked in court. When I (Megan) was called for jury duty in Rhode Island in 2017, I was selected for the voir dire process, during which potential jurors are questioned about their ability to follow the law and be fair. The case for which they were selecting a jury relied heavily on reports from witnesses. If my memory of this process is accurate—and we know that is a big if; studying memory does not make me immune from memory errors—we were told that our job was to determine if the witnesses were credible, and if a highly confident witness seemed credible, we should accept their testimony as accurate. In other words, our job was to determine who we thought was lying and who we thought was telling the truth. If we thought a witness was telling the truth, and they told us they were absolutely certain of their memory, then we should take their high confidence to be the same as high accuracy.

Memory research tells us that confidence does not mean accuracy, demonstrating one way in which our legal system is flawed in determining witness credibility. It is also important to note that while these memory qualities apply to everyone, not all individuals or members of groups have historically been considered equally credible in the legal system.[8] While members of marginalized communities are regularly not believed even when they are telling the truth, individuals with power and privilege are often believed even when they are, consciously or unconsciously, not telling the truth. This pattern can also be explained by understanding our memory systems. In earlier chapters, we introduced the idea of background knowledge and prior experience, and how these affect what we learn and remember (see Chapters 6 and 7). Our experiences, as well as what we hear from others and see in the media, shape our semantic memories and, in the same way, create stereotypes. The idea that certain groups are more trustworthy than others, and that certain types of people are "criminals", is deeply ingrained within our society[9, 10] and, as such, are ingrained in our cognitive networks, whether we want them there or not.

WITNESSING AND REPORTING A CRIME

We know that memory is reconstructed at the time of retrieval. But how is it that the reconstruction process leads to inaccuracies? One way is through receiving suggesting or misleading information. Importantly, this can occur very easily! Even the wording of questions asked can influence a witness' memory. For example, Elizabeth Loftus and John Palmer[11] had participants view a videotape of a car accident and then answer questions about it. In one question, Loftus and Palmer changed one word to imply either a low-speed or higher-speed accident. Some participants were asked, "How fast was the car going when it *contacted* the other car?" while others were asked, "How fast was the car going when it *smashed* the other car?" Participants gave higher speed estimates when the word *smashed* was used. One week later, the participants were asked a follow-up question, "Did you see any broken glass?" There was no broken glass in the video, but if the participants were asked about one car smashing into the other car, they were much more likely to falsely report broken glass. This experiment shows that even a single word within a single question can affect a person's memory for an event one week later.

People have falsely reported seeing a stop sign when they really saw a yield sign,[12] and have falsely reported being lost in a shopping mall when they were a child even though this never happened to them.[13] Memory mistakes can be made after a particularly stressful event, and even when accuracy should be particularly important for the witness.[14] In one study by Charles Morgan and colleagues, military personnel undergoing a POW camp exercise as part of Survival School training were asked to identify their interrogator.[14] As part of the experiment, some of the personnel were exposed to misleading information about what this person looked like, leading to misidentification of the interrogator once the exercise was over. Importantly, this occurred even though the military personnel are trained to resist this type of misinformation.

The circumstances of the crime itself can also affect how someone remembers the crime. For example, research suggests the presence of a weapon can draw attention of the eyewitness away from the perpetrator.[15] In this research, the presence of a weapon seems to lower how accurately the eyewitness can describe features of the perpetrator. However, overall the presence of a weapon does not seem to reduce an eyewitness' ability to correctly identify the perpetrator in a lineup. Still, lower accuracy in describing features of the perpetrator has the potential to lead law enforcement down the wrong path during an investigation. However, if the witness can then better describe the weapon that was present, this could help law enforcement more accurately identify the perpetrator. Thus the presence of a weapon does not always lead to worse memory for every aspect of the crime, or a net loss in useful information for law enforcement.

When a person witnesses a crime, it makes sense for law enforcement and other members of the community to want the witness to report as much as possible about what they saw. At the same time, we want the information to be accurate; false information can harm investigations and the people involved (e.g., a falsely accused suspect, future victims, etc.). Sometimes TV or movies show hypnosis as a way to draw out as many details as possible. However, hypnosis does not really provide a window to the event like it is portrayed in film. Instead, when an individual is hypnotized, they are highly suggestible and more likely to say more to the interviewer.[16] More details may come out during hypnosis, but there is no real way to tell whether these details are accurate or just guesses or inferences made by the witness. A much better option is the cognitive interview. The cognitive interview is an evidence-based protocol aimed to elicit as detailed and accurate an account as possible from a witness, and is considered a best practice.[17] During the cognitive interview, the interviewer asks open-ended questions to avoid inserting misinformation (e.g., "what did you see?" rather than "did you see the man run across the street?"). To try to increase the number of retrieval cues that the eyewitness can use to remember details from the event, the interviewer guides the eyewitness to reinstate the context in which the crime was witnessed. The interviewer asks the eyewitness to close their eyes and think about the physical context of the event, imagining themself at the crime scene and reporting what they see. The eyewitness is also encouraged to report as many details as possible, even if they seem small. Research shows the cognitive interview can increase the amount of accurately recalled information and limits the amount of inaccurate information reported.[17]

Adults' memories are far more susceptible to suggestion or misinformation than we tend to realize, but children are particularly susceptible to suggestion. Thus it is even more important with children to use evidence-based interviewing procedures. Research has shown that using open prompts, such as "tell me what happened" elicits memories from free recall, and the information elicited tends to be much more accurate than when more specific questions are asked.[18]

LINEUP PROCEDURES

Contrary to what crime shows may depict, DNA-rich evidence is only available in a small fraction of crimes, and eyewitnesses are still heavily relied upon within the legal system to identify culprits.[17] If a person witnesses a crime being committed by a person or people they know, then remembering details about who becomes relatively easy. The witness in this case may still be asked to remember other details of the crime, and these details are susceptible to memory errors and biases. However, when the witness does not know the culprit(s), issues related to identifying the culprit come front and center, and, unfortunately, remembering and subsequently recognizing unfamiliar faces is a particularly difficult task.

Faces are special to our visual systems, and we are particularly tuned to recognize that an object is a face. While there is a range of abilities across people (see Chapter 4), generally, memory for *specific unfamiliar* faces is difficult for most people. In fact, people tend to be poor at matching unfamiliar faces even when the two faces are presented simultaneously.[19] For example, people tend to be worse than one might expect at determining whether a person matches an official identification photo, such as one presented on a passport or even a higher-quality photo like you might find on a student ID, with one study finding accuracy to be only 75–79%.[20] And this task does not involve any remembering! Matching a face you saw some time ago from memory to one that you are viewing now, like in a lineup, adds another layer of difficulty that leads to even more errors. Further, it is particularly difficult to recognize faces outside of one's own ethnic group, sometimes called the cross-race effect. These effects have been well-documented in experimental laboratories and more realistic field studies.[21]

There are many factors that contribute to the accuracy of an eyewitness in identifying the culprit, including aspects of the crime, the crime scene, and the eyewitness themselves. Was it dark? Was the eyewitness close to the action, and did they have a good view? Was there a weapon? How good is the eyewitness' eyesight? Was the culprit the same race as the eyewitness? But in addition to all of this, the way that a lineup is administered can also affect identification accuracy.

A lineup is a form of recognition procedure in which a number of alternatives are presented, and the eyewitness' job is to identify the culprit or state that the culprit is not present. The lineup will be composed of one suspect, who may or may not be the culprit, and typically five fillers who are known by law enforcement to be innocent but are similar in appearance to the suspect. Law enforcement is interested in whether the eyewitness identifies the suspect as the culprit, presumably to use as evidence to convict the culprit. However, from an accuracy standpoint, there are two ways for lineup results to lead to the correct choice and two ways for the lineup to lead to the incorrect choice, illustrated in Figure 8.1. If the truth is

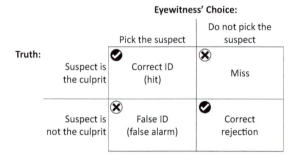

Figure 8.1 A depiction of the ways in which an eyewitness can be correct and incorrect during a lineup.

that the suspect is the culprit, then the eyewitness is correct if they identify the suspect. Cognitive psychologists call this a hit. The eyewitness is wrong if they do not identify the suspect, and this would be called a miss. However, the truth may also be that the suspect is not the culprit. In this case, if the eyewitness does not identify the suspect and instead states that the culprit is not present, then they are correct. This is called a correct rejection. (Note, in this case the eyewitness could also identify one of the fillers and be incorrect, but law enforcement knows that the fillers are innocent. Thus, the suspect should not be charged based on the lineup, and the lineup would not lead to the conviction of an innocent person.) If the eyewitness does identify the suspect, even though the suspect is innocent, then they have falsely identified the suspect. Cognitive psychologists call this a false alarm. Overall, the goal should be to increase both correct identifications and correct rejections, and in doing so, false alarms and misses will decrease. Some lineup procedures work well in doing this, while others tend to increase one type of error.

Based on decades of research, a team of senior eyewitness researchers led by Gary Wells compiled the best practices for collecting and preserving eyewitness identification evidence. Published in 2020, the result was nine recommendations to help increase the reliability and integrity of eyewitness evidence.[17] Some of these recommendations involve methods of conducting the lineup to improve accuracy.

For example, one relatively easy way to reduce false identifications during lineups is to provide a warning to the eyewitness that the person who committed the crime may not be present in the lineup. Many eyewitnesses believe, falsely, that the police must have strong evidence if they are being asked to make an identification from a lineup, and many believe the culprit is likely to be in the lineup. The recommendation to inform the eyewitness that "none of these" or "I don't know" is an option makes it less likely that the eyewitness will pick the person from the lineup who looks the closest. For example, in an experiment conducted by Wells,[22] witnesses viewed a lineup that contained the culprit, and 54% picked the culprit while 21% made no choice. Thus when the culprit was removed from the lineup, it would make sense that most people in the experiment would then make no choice; logically, if 54% could correctly identify the culprit, then this share of people should join the other 21% in making no choice when the correct answer was no choice. However, instead of 75% accuracy (54+21), only 32% of people made no choice when the culprit was not present. The remainder of people incorrectly selected a different photo.

The researchers recommend that repeated identifications be avoided with the same suspect. Repeated identifications do not make an eyewitness identification more reliable but, instead, serve to contaminate the eyewitness' memory. If the eyewitness sees the suspect in the first lineup, they now are more likely to look familiar during any subsequent identification procedure, introducing the possibility that the eyewitness will make a source memory error (i.e., thinking they look familiar because they are the culprit, and not because they have been seen in a lineup before). Repeated identifications can also make the eyewitness feel more confident in their decision, and inflating their confidence does not make it more likely that they are accurate.

Another recommendation is to conduct the lineup in a double-blind fashion.[17] This means neither the person conducting the lineup (likely a law enforcement officer) nor the witness knows who the suspect is. Doing so helps prevent confirmatory feedback that may inflate the confidence of the eyewitness, and avoids any subtle cues that might lead the eyewitness to be more likely to identify the suspect than any of the other fillers, other than from their memory alone.

Similarly, they recommend that lineups only include one suspect and are constructed with five fillers that do not make the suspect stand out to avoid making it more likely that the eyewitness identifies the suspect from any cue other than their memory.[17] One specific example that violates this recommendation, and is explicitly discouraged whenever possible, is the showup. In this situation, the eyewitness is presented with a single individual and asked to state whether or not this person committed the crime. We already discussed in this chapter that our memories are susceptible to suggestion, and this is a situation in which the suggestion that the suspect is the culprit seems glaringly clear.

The remaining recommendations include conducting pre-lineup interviews to collect as much detailed information from the eyewitness as possible, and instructing the witness not to discuss the crime with anyone else.[17] They recommend taking confidence statements from the witnesses right after a lineup decision is made (whether they pick the suspect or not), to video-record all procedures and interviews, and to ensure that there is evidence-based grounds to conduct a lineup in the first place.

It is difficult, if not impossible, to perfectly preserve an eyewitness' memory of a crime. However, by understanding how memory works and implementing best practices recommended by memory and eyewitness researchers, law enforcement can help reduce memory errors leading to miscarriages of justice.

CONCLUSION: CAN WE BELIEVE EYEWITNESSES?

The accuracy of our memories, and our confidence in them, is possibly never more impactful than when dealing with the law. Memories are rarely perfect accounts of the past and are not designed to be that way. What does this mean for the legal system? Can we ever believe eyewitnesses?

In closing this chapter, we want to address a critical issue that often comes up when discussing memory and legal system implications. That is, do eyewitnesses always come with reasonable doubt? Learning about case after case in which eyewitnesses were confidently inaccurate, and how easy it can be to alter our memories, it may seem like we should never believe eyewitnesses and, instead, require physical evidence. Even worse, some may perceive the information presented in this chapter as grounds to take away a victim's voice, and we certainly do not want that.

On the contrary, we believe understanding how memory works, that it is reconstructive and susceptible to errors, means we should be tolerant when witnesses or victims have holes in their memories or get details wrong. These memory errors do not mean the victim is lying! Take Thompson's case. She *was* raped, and many of the details from her recollection were accurate. While her particular memory error ultimately had large negative consequences for Cotton, we know that facial recognition is particularly difficult, and Poole's photograph was not in the original lineup for her to select.

Another example comes from Christine Blasey Ford. Her report of being sexually assaulted by Brett Kavanaugh, now a US Supreme Court Justice, was incredibly detailed. Importantly, while there were some gaps and inconsistencies in some of the peripheral details, the main points of her story did not waiver. Her memories are exactly what we would expect from a victim who is telling the truth, once we know how memory works.[23] Creating elaborate memories that are completely false is not impossible but is extremely uncommon and would require the person to be in a highly suggestible state with repeated questioning and attempts to draw out details.

Together, these two cases also provide examples of who we tend to believe and who we do not. Cotton was a wrongly convicted black man who claimed his innocence from the beginning yet was not believed; he fits the stereotype that black men rape white women.[9, 10]

In contrast, Kavanaugh is a powerful white man, and he was believed despite Blasey Ford's convincing testimony.

Of course, allowing innocent people to go to prison for crimes they did not commit is horrendous. Silencing victims is also horrendous. These issues are certainly not easy, but we believe that by better understanding how memory works and applying science to the legal system, we can hopefully reduce both of these outcomes.

FURTHER READING

BOOKS AND ARTICLES

An overview of memory and the common errors we make: Schacter, D. L. (2021). *The seven sins of memory: How the mind forgets and remembers* (updated ed.). Mariner Books.

Jill Price's personal account of being unable to forget: Price, J. (2009). *The woman who can't forget: The extraordinary story of living with the most remarkable memory known to science—A memoir.* Simon & Schuster.

Joshua Foer's foray into memory championships: Foer, J. (2011). *Moonwalking with Einstein: The art and science of remembering everything.* The Penguin Press.

An engaging and detailed story of amnesic patient H.M.: Hilts, P. J. (1995). *Memory's ghost: The nature of memory and the strange tale of Mr. M.* Touchstone.

An overview of trauma and memory research: McNally, R. J. (2003). *Remembering trauma.* Belknap Press/Harvard University Press.

Books on improving learning and memory in educational settings:

Brown, A., & Kaminske, A. N. (2018). *Five teaching and learning myths debunked: A guide for teachers.* Routledge. https://doi.org/10.4324/9781315150239

Brown, P. C., Roediger, H. L., & McDaniel, M. A. (2014). *Make it stick: The science of successful learning.* Belknap Press/Harvard University Press. https://doi.org/10.2307/j.ctt6wprs3

Sumeracki, M. A., Nebel, C. L., Kuepper-Tetzel, C. E., & Kaminske, A. N. (2023). *Ace that test: A student's guide to learning better* (K. Tiller, Illus.). Routledge. https://doi.org/10.4324/9781003327530

Weinstein, Y., & Sumeracki, M. A. (2019). *Understanding how we learn: A visual guide* (O. Caviglioli, Illus.). Routledge. https://doi.org/10.4324/97 80203710463

A condensed guide on science of learning principles: Deans for Impact. (2015). *The science of learning.* https://www.deansforimpact.org/tools-and-resources/ the-science-of-learning

Jennifer Thompson and Ronald Cotton's joint memoir: Thompson-Cannino, J., Cotton, R., & Torneo, E. (2009). *Picking Cotton: Our memoir of injustice and redemption.* St. Martin's Press. https://doi.org/10.1177/17438721110070021103

A compilation of recommendations from memory researchers to law enforcement: Wells, G. L., Kovera, M. B., Douglass, A. B., Brewer, N., Meissner, C. A., & Wixted, J. T. (2020). Policy and procedure recommendations for the collection and preservation of eyewitness identification evidence. *Law and Human Behavior, 44*(1), 3–36. https://doi.org/10.1037/lhb0000359

YOUTUBE VIDEOS AND TED TALKS

TED Talk by Peter Doolittle covering working memory: Doolittle, P. (2013, June). *How your "working memory" makes sense of the world* [Video]. TED Conferences. https://www.ted.com/talks/peter_doolittle_how_your_working_memory_ makes_sense_of_the_world?

ABC News Interview with Jill Price, the woman who can't forget: ABC News. (2008, May 17). *The woman that never forgets—Jill Price first interview!* [Video]. YouTube. https://youtu.be/aAbQvmf0YOQ?si=o2cxzp9kleNv16zo

TED Talk by Joshua Foer, the science writer who "accidentally" won the U.S. Memory Championship: Foer, J. (2012, February). *Feats of memory anyone can do* [Video]. TED Conferences. https://www.ted.com/talks/ joshua_foer_feats_of_memory_anyone_can_do?

Series of videos with K.C., an amnesiac patient studied by Endel Tulving: Habib, R. (2006, June 28). *KC1* [Video]. YouTube. https://youtu.be/ tXHk0a3RvLc?si=RpRjEPQlhVLMojEy

Habib, R. (2006, June 28). *KC2* [Video]. YouTube. https://youtu.be/ Ai2Ir1HpO0Y?si=XUu_9NqxWJjkl28D

Habib R. (2006, June 28). *KC3* [Video]. YouTube. https://youtu.be/ mvWjahGfONk?si=DLPv6UF9bcTgYG52

TED Talk by Elizabeth Loftus covering confidence and false memories: Loftus, E. (2013, September). *How reliable is your memory?* [Video]. TED Conferences. https://www.ted.com/talks/elizabeth_loftus_how_reliable_is_your_memory?

Interviews with Jennifer Thompson and Ronald Cotton, with input from memory researchers Elizabeth Loftus and Gary Wells about the case:

> CBS News. (2009, March 9). *Eyewitness testimony part 1* [Video]. YouTube. https://youtu.be/u-SBTRLoPuo
>
> CBS News. (2009, March 8). *Eyewitness testimony part 2* [Video]. YouTube. https://youtu.be/I4V6aoYuDcg

AUTHOR'S WEBSITE

For free resources on effective learning and remembering, including downloadable materials such as posters, slides, and bookmarks, a blog, and a podcast, visit *The Learning Scientists* at https://learningscientists.org

OTHER WEBSITES

Alzheimer's Association. https://www.alz.org/

> For an explanation of how Alzheimer's changes the brain, see this page: https://www.alz.org/alzheimers-dementia/what-is-alzheimers/brain_tour_part_2

The Innocence Project. https://innocenceproject.org/

Retrieval Practice. https://retrievalpractice.org

REFERENCES

CHAPTER 1

1. Price, J. (2009). *The woman who can't forget: The extraordinary story of living with the most remarkable memory known to science—A memoir*. Simon & Schuster.

2. Nairne, J. S., Thompson, S. R., & Pandeirada, J. N. S. (2007). Adaptive memory: Survival processing enhances retention. *Journal of Experimental Psychology: Learning, Memory, and Cognition, 33*(2), 263–273. https://doi.org/10.1037/0278-7393.33.2.263

3. Clayton, N. S., Yu, K. S., & Dickinson, A. (2001). Scrub jays (Aphelocoma coerulescens) form integrated memories of their multiple features of caching episodes. *Journal of Experimental Psychology: Animal Behavior Process, 27*(1), 17–29. https://doi.org/10.1037/0097-7403.27.1.17

4. Cowles, H. M. (2020). *The scientific method: An evolution of thinking from Darwin to Dewey*. Harvard University Press.

5. Hothersall, D., & Lovett, B. J. (2022). *History of psychology* (5th ed.). Cambridge University Press.

6. McDermott, J. J. (1967). *The writings of William James*. Random House, Inc.

7. James, W. (1890). *The principles of psychology* (2 Vols.). Henry Holt.

8. James, W. (1899). *Talks to teachers on psychology and to students on some of life's ideals*. Henry Holt.

9. Ebbinghaus, H. (1964). *Memory: A contribution to experimental psychology*. Dover. (Original work published 1885)

10. Boring, E. G. (1950). *A history of experimental psychology* (2nd ed.). Appleton-Century-Crofts.

11. James, W. (1884). Some omissions of introspective psychology. *Mind, 9*, 1–26.

12. Calkins, M. W. (1896). Association (II.). *Psychological Review, 3*(1), 32–49. https://doi.org/10.1037/h0068098

13. Calkins, M. W. (1906). A reconciliation between structural and functional psychology. *Psychological Review, 13*(2), 61–81. https://doi.org/10.1037/h0071994

14. Watson, J. B. (1936). John Broadus Watson. In C. Murchison (Ed.), *A history of psychology in autobiography* (Vol. 3, pp. 271–281). Russel & Russel.

15. Watson, J. B. (1913). Psychology as the behaviorist views it. *Psychological Review, 20*(2), 158–177. https://doi.org/10.1037/h0074428

16. DeAngelis, T. (2010, January). 'Little Albert' regains his identity. *Monitor on Psychology, 41*(1). https://www.apa.org/monitor/2010/01/little-albert

17. Skinner, B. F. (1938). *The behavior of organisms: An experimental analysis.* Appleton-Century.

18. Bartlett, F. C. (1932). *Remembering: A study in experimental and social psychology.* Cambridge University Press.

19. Skinner, B. F. (1957). *Verbal behavior.* Appleton-Century-Crofts. https://doi.org/10.1037/11256-000

20. Gardner, H. (1985). *The mind's new science: A history of the cognitive revolution.* Basic Books.

21. Hebb, D. O. (1949). *The organization of behavior: A neuropsychological theory.* Wiley.

22. Miller, G. A. (1956). The magical number seven, plus or minus two: Some limits on our capacity for processing information. *Psychological Review, 63*(2), 81–97. https://doi.org/10.1037/h0043158

23. Neisser, U. (1967). *Cognitive psychology.* Appleton-Century-Crofts.

24. Roediger, H. L. (2004, March 1). What happened to behaviorism. *APS Observer, 17*(3). https://www.psychologicalscience.org/observer/what-happened-to-behaviorism

CHAPTER 2

1. Jenkins, J. J. (1979). Four points to remember: A tetrahedral model of memory experiments. In L. S. Cermak & F. I. M. Craik (Eds.), *Levels of processing in human memory* (pp. 429–446). Erlbaum.

2. Roediger, H. L. (2008). Relativity of remembering: Why the laws of memory vanished. *Annual Review of Psychology, 59*, 225–254. https://doi.org/10.1146/annurev.psych.57.102904.190139

3. Tulving, E. (2007). Are there 256 different kinds of memory? In J. S. Nairne (Ed.), *The foundations of remembering: Essays in honor of Henry L. Roediger, III* (pp. 39–52). Psychology Press.

4. Miller, G. A. (1956). The magical number seven, plus or minus two: Some limits on our capacity for processing information. *Psychological Review*, 63(2), 81–97. https://doi.org/10.1037/h0043158

5. Baddeley, A. (2012). Working memory: Theories, models, and controversies. *Annual Review of Psychology*, 63, 1–29. https://doi.org/10.1146/annurev-psych-120710-100422

6. Roediger, H. L., Zaromb, F., & Lin, W. (2017). A typology of memory terms. In J. H. Byrne (Ed.), *Learning and memory: A comprehensive reference* (2nd ed., pp. 7–19). Academic Press. http://doi.org/10.1016/B978-0-12-809324-5.21003-1

7. Maquet, P. (2001). The role of sleep in learning and memory. *Science*, 294(5544), 1048–1052. https://doi.org/10.1126/science.1062856

8. Loftus, E. (2013, June). *How reliable is your memory?* [Video]. TED Conferences. https://www.ted.com/talks/elizabeth_loftus_how_reliable_is_your_memory

9. Tulving, E. (1983). *Elements of episodic memory*. Oxford University Press.

10. Ebbinghaus, H. (1964). *Memory: A contribution to experimental psychology*. Dover. (Original work published 1885)

11. Warrington, E. K., & Weiskrantz, L. (1970). Amnesic syndrome: Consolidation or retrieval? *Nature*, 228, 628–630. https://doi.org/10.1038/228628a0

12. National Highway Traffic Safety Administration. (n.d.). *You can help prevent hot car deaths: Tips for keeping children safe.* https://www.nhtsa.gov/child-safety/you-can-help-prevent-hot-car-deaths

13. Hallford, D. J., Barry, T. J., Austin, D. W., Raes, F., Takano, K., & Klein, B. (2020). Impairments in episodic future thinking for positive events and anticipatory pleasure in major depression. *Journal of Affective Disorders*, 260, 536–543. https://doi.org/10.1016/j.jad.2019.09.039

CHAPTER 3

1. Kisilevsky, B. S., Hains, S. M., Lee, K., Xie, X., Huang, H., Ye, H. H., Zhang, K., & Wang, Z. (2003). Effects of experience on fetal voice recognition. *Psychological Science*, 14(3), 220–224. https://doi.org/10.1111/1467-9280.02435

2. Rovee-Collier, C., & Cuevas, K. (2009). Multiple memory systems are unnecessary to account for infant memory development: An ecological model. *Developmental Psychology*, 45(1), 160–174. https://doi.org/10.1037/a0014538

3. Bearce, K. H., & Rovee-Collier, C. (2006). Repeated priming increases memory accessibility in infants. *Journal of Experimental Child Psychology*, 93(4), 357–376. https://doi.org/10.1016/j.jecp.2005.10.002

4. Gathercole, S. E. (1998). The development of memory. *Journal of Child Psychology and Psychiatry*, 39(1), 3–27. https://pubmed.ncbi.nlm.nih.gov/9534084/

5. Gathercole, S. E., Pickering, S. J., Ambridge, B., & Wearing, H. (2004). The structure of working memory from 4 to 15 years of age. *Developmental Psychology*, 40(2), 177–190. https://doi.org/10.1037/0012-1649.40.2.177

6. Peterson, C., Sales, J. M., Rees, M., & Fivush, R. (2007). Parent-child talk and children's memory for stressful events. *Applied Cognitive Psychology*, 21(8), 1057–1075. https://doi.org/10.1002/acp.1314

7. Peterson, C., & Whalen, N. (2001). Five years later: Children's memory for medical emergencies. *Applied Cognitive Psychology*, 15, S7–S24. https://doi.org/10.1002/acp.832

8. Berry, B. M., Miller, L. R., Berns, M., & Kucewicz, M. (2023). The possibility of eidetic memory in a patient report of epileptogenic zone in right temporo-parietal-occipital cortex. *Life*, 13(4), 956. https://doi.org/10.3390/life13040956

9. Tessler, M., & Nelson, K. (1994). Making memories: The influence of joint encoding on later recall by young children. *Consciousness and Cognition*, 3(3–4), 307–326. https://doi.org/10.1006/ccog.1994.1018

10. Pillemer, D. B., & White, S. H. (1989). Childhood events recalled by children and adults. In H. W. Reese (Ed.), *Advances in child development and behavior* (Vol. 21, pp. 297–340). Academic Press. https://doi.org/10.1016/S0065-2407(08)60280-3

11. Schacter, D. L. (1999). The seven sins of memory: Insights from psychology and cognitive neuroscience. *American Psychologist*, 54(3), 182–203. https://doi.org/10.1037/0003-066X.54.3.182

12. Newcombe, N., & Fox, N. A. (1994). Infantile amnesia: Through a glass darkly. *Child Development*, 65(1), 31–40. https://doi.org/10.2307/1131363

13. Conway, M. A., Wang, Q., Hanyu, K., & Haque, S. (2005). A cross-cultural investigation of autobiographical memory: On the universality and cultural variation of the reminiscence bump. *Journal of Cross-Cultural Psychology*, 36(6), 739–749. https://doi.org/10.1177/0022022105280512

14. Hartshorne, J. K., & Germine, L. T. (2015). When does cognitive functioning peak? The asynchronous rise and fall of different cognitive abilities across the life span. *Psychological Science*, 26(4), 433–443. https://doi.org/10.1177/0956797614567339

15. Craik, F. I. M., & Rose, N. S. (2012). Memory encoding and aging: A neurocognitive perspective. *Neuroscience and Biobehavioral Reviews*, 36, 1729–1739. https://doi.org/10.1016/j.neubiorev.2011.11.007

16. Dixon, R. A., & Cohen, A. L. (2003). Cognitive development in adulthood. In R. M. Lerner, M. A. Easterbrooks, & J. Mistry (Eds.), *Handbook of psychology: Vol. 6. Developmental psychology* (pp. 443–461). Wiley.

17. Global Health Observatory. (2020). *Life expectancy and healthy life expectancy: Data by country* [Data set]. World Health Organization. https://apps.who.int/gho/data/node.main.688

18. Sander, M. C., Lindenberger, U., & Werkle-Bergner, M. (2012). Lifespan age differences in working memory: A two-component framework. *Neuroscience and Biobehavioral Reviews*, 36(6), 2007–2033. https://doi.org/10.1016/j.neubiorev.2012.06.004

19. Old, S. R., & Naveh-Benjamin, M. (2012). Age differences in memory for names: The effect of pre-learned semantic associations. *Psychology and Aging*, 27(2), 462–473. https://doi.org/10.1037/a0025194

20. Nyberg, L., Lövdén, M., Riklund, K., Lindenberger, U., & Bäckman, L. (2012). Memory aging and brain maintenance. *Trends in Cognitive Science*, 16(5), 292–305. https://doi.org/10.1016/j.tics.2012.04.005

21. Salthouse, T. A. (2017). Contributions of the individual differences approach to cognitive aging. *Journals of Gerontology: Psychological Sciences*, 72(1), 7–15. https://doi.org/10.1093/geronb/gbw069

22. Maquet, P. (2001). The role of sleep in learning and memory. *Science*, 294(5544), 1048–1052. https://doi.org/10.1126/science.1062856

23. Killgore, W. D. (2010). Effects of sleep deprivation on cognition. *Progress in Brain Research*, 185, 105–129. https://doi.org/10.1016/B978-0-444-53702-7.00007-5

24. Zhang, R. C., & Madan, C. R. (2021). How does caffeine influence memory? Drug, experimental, and demographic factors. *Neuroscience and Biobehavioral Reviews*, 131, 525–538. https://doi.org/10.1016/j.neubiorev.2021.09.033

25. Li, J., Vitiello, M. V., & Gooneratne, N. S. (2018). Sleep in normal aging. *Sleep Medicine Clinics*, 13(1), 1–11. https://doi.org/10.1016/j.jsmc.2017.09.001

26. Wu-Chung, E. L., Leal, S. L., Denny, B. T., Cheng, S. L., & Fagundes, C. P. (2022). Spousal caregiving, widowhood, and cognition: A systematic review and a biopsychosocial framework for understanding the relationship between interpersonal losses and dementia risk in older adulthood. *Neuroscience and Biobehavioral Reviews*, 134, 104487. https://doi.org/10.1016/j.neubiorev.2021.12.010

27. Alzheimer's Disease International. (2021). *World Alzheimer report 2021: Journey through the diagnosis of dementia.* https://www.alzint.org/u/World-Alzheimer-Report-2021.pdf

28. How is Alzheimer's disease treated? (2023, September 12). *National Institute on Aging*. Retrieved October 6, 2023, from https://www.nia.nih.gov/health/how-alzheimers-disease-treated

CHAPTER 4

1. Van Sant, G. (Director). (1997). *Good will hunting* [Film]. Be Gentlemen; Miramax Films.

2. Rhimes, S., Pompeo, E., Heinberg, A., Reaser, A., Beers, B., Allen, D., Parriott, J. D., Renshaw, J., Rafner, J., Rater, J., Hodder, K., Vernhoff, K., Gordon, M., Wilding, M., Noxon, M., Marinis, M., Horton, P., Corn, R., McKee, S.,. . . Clack, Z. (Executive Producers). (2005–present). *Grey's anatomy* [TV series]. Shondaland Entertainment One; ABC.

3. Gordon, M., Davis, J., Bernero, E. A., Spera, D., Mundy, C., Mirren, S., Messer, E., Barrois, J. S., Frazier, B., Bring, H., & Kershaw, G. (Executive Producers). (2005–present). *Criminal minds* [TV series]. Entertainment One; Erica Messer Productions; ABC Signature; CBS Studios.

4. Franks, S., Henze, C., Kulchak, K., Damski, M., & Callahan, B. (Executive Producers). (2006–2014). *Psych* [TV series]. USA Network.

5. Baxendale, S. (2004). Memories aren't made of this: Amnesia at the movies. *British Medical Journal, 329*(7480), 1480–1483. https://doi.org/10.1136/bmj.329.7480.1480

6. International Association of Memory. (n.d.). *Speed cards*. https://iam-stats.org/discipline.php?id=SPDCARDS

7. Foer, J. (2011). *Moonwalking with Einstein: The art and science of remembering everything*. The Penguin Press.

8. Foer, J. (2012, February). *Feats of memory anyone can do* [Video]. TED Conferences. https://www.ted.com/talks/joshua_foer_feats_of_memory_anyone_can_do?language=en

9. Berry, B. M., Miller, L. R., Berns, M., & Kucewicz, M. (2023). The possibility of eidetic memory in a patient report of epileptogenic zone in right temporo-parietal-occiptal cortex. *Life, 13*, 956. https://doi.org/10.3390/life13040956

10. Borges, J. L. (1964). *Labyrinths* (J. E. Irby, Trans.). New Directions. (Original work published 1944)

11. Santangelo, V., Cavallinoa, C., Paola, C., Santori, A., Macrì, S., McGaugh, J. L., & Campolongo, P. (2018). Enhanced brain activity associated with memory access

in highly superior autobiographical memory. *The Proceedings of the National Academy of Sciences*, 115(30), 7795–7800. https://doi.org/10.1073/pnas.1802730115

12. Price, J. (2009). *The woman who can't forget: The extraordinary story of living with the most remarkable memory known to science—A memoir.* Simon & Schuster.

13. Santangelo, V., Pedale, T., Colucci, P., Giuliettie, G., Macrì, S., & Campolongo, P. (2021). Highly superior autobiographical memory in aging: A single case study. *Cortex*, 143, 267–280. https://doi.org/10.1016/j.cortex.2021.05.011

14. Park, H. O. (2023). Autism spectrum disorder and savant syndrome: A systematic literature review. *Journal of Korean Academy of Child and Adolescent Psychiatry*, 34(2), 76–92. https://doi.org/10.5765/jkacap.230003

15. Russell, R., Duchaine, B., & Nakayama, K. (2009). Super-recognizers: People with extraordinary face recognition ability. *Psychonomic Bulletin & Review*, 16(2), 252–257. https://doi.org/10.3758/PBR.16.2.252

16. Megreya, A. M., & Burton, A. M. (2008). Matching faces to photographs: Poor performance in eyewitness memory (without the memory). *Journal of Experimental Psychology: Applied*, 14(4), 364–372. https://doi.org/10.1037/a0013464

17. Liman, D. (Director). (2002). *The Bourne identity* [Film]. Universal Pictures.

18. Kopelman, M. D. (2002). Disorders of memory. *Brain*, 125, 2152–2190. https://doi.org/10.1093/brain/awf229

19. Broggi, M., & Ready, R. (2021). Academic skills, self-perceptions, and grades in university students with a history of multiple concussions: The mediating roles of processing speed and psychological symptoms. *The Clinical Neuropsychologist*, 36(8), 2188–2204. https://doi.org/10.1080/13854046.2021.1958924

20. Agenagnew, L., Tesfaye, E., Alemayehu, S., Masane, M., Bete, T., & Tadessa, J. (2020). Dissociative amnesia with dissociative fugue and psychosis: A case report from a 25-year-old Ethiopian woman. *Case Reports in Psychiatry*, 1–7. https://doi.org/10.1155/2020/3281487

21. Kaplan, K., & Hunsberger, H. C. (2023). Benzodiazepine-induced anterograde amnesia: Detrimental side effect to novel study tool. *Frontiers in Pharmacology*, 14, 1257030. https://doi.org/10.3389/fphar.2023.1257030

22. Rensen, Y. C. M., Oosterman, J. M., Eling, P. A. T. M., & Kessels, R. P. C. (2022). "Cinderella was attacked by the big bad wolf, but the police saved her": Intrusions and confabulations on story recall in Korsakoff's syndrome and alcohol-related cognitive impairments. *Cognitive Neuropsychiatry*, 28(2), 85–101. https://doi.org/10.1080/13546805.2022.2153658

23. Moscovitch, M. (1989). Confabulation and the frontal systems: Strategic versus associative retrieval in neuropsychological theories of memory. In H. L. Roediger & F. I. Craik (Eds.), *Varieties of memory and consciousness: Essays in honor of Endel Tulving* (pp. 13–160). Lawrence Erlbaum.

24. White, A. M. (2003). What happened? Alcohol, memory blackouts, and the brain. *Alcohol Research & Health*, 27(2), 186–196. https://pubmed.ncbi.nlm.nih.gov/15303630

25. Alzheimer's Disease International. (2021). *World Alzheimer report 2021: Journey through the diagnosis of dementia*. https://www.alzint.org/u/World-Alzheimer-Report-2021.pdf

26. Doctrow, B. (2023, January 10). *Blood test for early Alzheimer's detection*. NIH Research Matters. https://www.nih.gov/news-events/nih-research-matters/blood-test-early-alzheimer-s-detection

27. Harris, T. (2006). *Hannibal rising*. Delacorte Press.

28. Segal, P. (Director). (2004). *50 first dates* [Film]. Columbia Pictures; Happy Madison Productions; Anonymous Content; Flower Films.

CHAPTER 5

1. Kensinger, E. A., & Schacter, D. L. (2016). Memory and emotion. In L. F. Barrett, M. Lewis, & J. M. Haviland-Jones (Eds.), *Handbook of emotions* (4th ed., pp. 564–578). The Guilford Press.

2. Peterson, C., & Whalen, N. (2001). Five years later: Children's memory for medical emergencies. *Applied Cognitive Psychology*, 15, S7–S24. https://doi.org/10.1002/acp.832

3. Kocab, K., & Sporer, S. L. (2016). The weapon focus effect for person identification and descriptions: A meta-analysis. In M. K. Miller & B. H. Bornstein (Eds.), *Advances in psychology and law* (pp. 71–117). Springer International Publishing. https://doi.org/10.1007/978-3-319-29406-3_3

4. Kensinger, E. A., & Corkin, S. (2004). Two routes to emotional memory: Distinct neural processes for valence and arousal. *Proceedings of the National Academy of Sciences*, 101(9), 3310–3315. https://doi.org/10.1073/pnas.0306408101

5. Kensinger, E. A., & Schacter, D. L. (2006). When the Red Sox shocked the Yankees: Comparing negative and positive memories. *Psychonomic Bulletin and Review*, 13, 757–763. https://doi.org/10.3758/BF03193993

6. Breslin, C. W., & Safer, M. A. (2011). Effects of event valence on long-term memory for two baseball championship games. *Psychological Science*, 22(11), 1408–1412. https://doi.org/10.1177/0956797611419171

7. Kensinger, E. A., & Ford, J. H. (2020). Retrieval of emotional events from memory. *Annual Review of Psychology*, 71, 251–272. https://doi.org/10.1146/annurev-psych-010419-051123

8. Brown, R., & Kulik, J. (1977). Flashbulb memories. *Cognition*, 5, 73–99.

9. DeSoto, K. A., & Roediger, H. L. (2014). Positive and negative correlations between confidence and accuracy for the same events in recognition of categorized lists. *Psychological Science*, 25(3), 781–788. https://doi.org/10.1177/0956797613516149

10. Neisser, U., & Harsch, N. (1992). Phantom flashbulbs: False recollections of hearing the news about Challenger. In E. Winograd & U. Neisser (Eds.), *Affect and accuracy in recall: Studies of 'fashbulb' memories* (Emory Symposia in Cognition, pp. 9–31). Cambridge University Press. https://doi.org/10.1017/CBO9780511664069.003

11. Hirst, W., Phelps, E. A., Meksin, R., Vaidya, C. J., Johnson, M. K., Mitchell, K. J., Buckner, R. L., Budson, A. E., Gabrieli, J. D. E., Lustig, C., Mather, M., Ochsner, K. N., Schacter, D., Simons, J. S., Lyle, K. B., Cuc, A. F., & Olsson, A. (2015). A ten-year follow-up study of memory for the attack of September 11, 2001: Flashbulb memories and memories for flashbulb events. *Journal of Experimental Psychology: General*, 144(3), 604–623. https://doi.org/10.1037/xge0000055

12. American Psychiatric Association. (1980). *Diagnostic and statistical manual of mental disorders* (3rd ed.). APA Press.

13. American Psychiatric Association. (2022). Trauma- and stressor-related disorders. In *Diagnostic and statistical manual of mental disorders* (5th ed., text rev.). APA Press. https://doi.org/10.1176/appi.books.9780890425787

14. May, C. L., & Wisco, B. E. (2016). Defining trauma: How level of exposure and proximity affect risk for posttraumatic stress disorder. *Psychological Trauma: Theory, Research, Practice, and Policy*, 8(2), 233–240. https://doi.org/10.1037/tra0000077

15. Dalenberg, C. J., Straus, E., & Carlson, E. B. (2017). Defining trauma. In S. N. Gold (Ed.), *APA handbook of trauma psychology: Foundations in knowledge* (Vol. 1, pp. 15–33). American Psychological Association. https://doi.org/10.1037/0000019-002

16. McNally, R. J. (2003). *Remembering trauma*. Belknap Press/Harvard University Press.

17. Schacter, D. L. (1999). The seven sins of memory: Insights from psychology and cognitive neuroscience. *American Psychologist*, 54(3), 182–203. https://doi.org/10.1037//0003-066x.54.3.182

18. Barlow, M. R., Pezdek, K., & Blandón-Gitlin, I. (2017). Trauma and memory. In S. N. Gold (Ed.), *APA handbook of trauma psychology: Foundations in knowledge* (Vol. 1, pp. 307–331). American Psychological Association. https://doi.org/10.1037/0000019-016

19. Shields, G. S., Sazma, M. A., McCullough, A. M., & Yonelinas, A. P. (2017). The effects of acute stress on episodic memory: A meta-analysis and integrative review. *Psychological Bulletin*, 143(6), 636–675. https://doi.org/10.1037/bul0000100

CHAPTER 6

1. Witherby, A. E., & Carpenter, S. K. (2022). The rich-get-richer effect: Prior knowledge predicts new learning of domain-relevant information. *Journal of Experimental Psychology: Learning, Memory, and Cognition*, 48(4), 483–498. https://doi.org/10.1037/xlm0000996

2. Kintsch, W. (1988). The role of knowledge in discourse comprehension: A construction-integration model. *Psychological Review*, 95(2), 163–182. https://doi.org/10.1037/0033-295X.95.2.163

3. Hidi, S., & Renninger, K. A. (2006). The four-phase model of interest development. *Educational Psychologist*, 41(2), 111–127. https://doi.org/10.1207/s15326985ep4102_4

4. Asher, S. R., Hymel, S., & Wigfield, A. (1978). Influence of topic interest on children's reading comprehension. *Journal of Reading Behavior*, 10(1), 35–47. https://doi.org/10.1080/10862967809547253

5. Kenny, C., & Henn, S. (Hosts). (2014, October 17). When women stopped coding (No. 576) [Audio podcast episode]. In *Planet Money*. National Public Radio. https://www.npr.org/sections/money/2016/07/22/487069271/episode-576-when-women-stopped-coding

6. Margolis, J., Fisher, A., & Miller, F. (2000). The anatomy of interest: Women in undergraduate computer science. *Women's Studies Quarterly*, 28(1/2), 104–127. https://www.jstor.org/stable/40004448

7. Maquet, P. (2001). The role of sleep in learning and memory. *Science*, 294(5544), 1048–1052. https://doi.org/10.1126/science.1062856

8. Park, K. S., Zaplatosch, M. E., Wahlheim, C. N., Etnier, J. L., Wideman, L., & Adams, W. M. (2021). Effect of mild dehydration on episodic memory and inhibitory control in college-aged young adults. *Medicine & Science in Sports & Exercise*, 53(8S), 312. https://doi.org/10.1249/01.mss.0000762780.54834.dc

9. Rączy, K., & Orzechowski, J. (2021). When working memory is in a mood: Combined effects of induced affect and processing of emotional words. *Current Psychology*, 40, 2843–2852. https://doi.org/10.1007/s12144-019-00208-x

10. Ericsson, K. A., & Kintsch, W. (1995). Long-term working memory. *Psychological Review*, 102(2), 211–245.

11. Azcue, N., Gómez-Esteban, J. C., Acera, M., Tijero, B., Ayo-Mentxakatorre, N., Pérez-Concha, T., Murueta-Goyena, A., Lafuente, J. V., Prada, Á., López de Munain, A., Ruiz-Irastorza, G., Ribacoba, L., Gabilondo, I., & Del Pino, R. (2022). Brain fog of post-COVID-19 condition and chronic fatigue syndrome, same medical disorder? *Journal of Translational Medicine*, 20, 569. https://doi.org/10.1186/s12967-022-03764-2

12. Sweller, J., & Chandler, P. (1994). Why some material is difficult to learn. *Cognition and Instruction*, 12(3), 185–233. https://doi.org/10.1207/s1532690xci1203_1

13. Dunlosky, J., Rawson, K. A., Marsh, E. J., Nathan, M. J., & Willingham, D. T. (2013). Improving students' learning with effective learning techniques: Promising directions from cognitive and educational psychology. *Psychological Science in the Public Interest*, 14(1), 4–58. https://doi.org/10.1177/1529100612453266

14. Roediger, H. L., Putnam, A. L., & Smith, M. A. (2011). Ten benefits of testing and their applications to educational practice. In J. P. Mestre & B. H. Ross (Eds.), *The psychology of learning and motivation: Cognition in education* (pp. 1–36). Elsevier Academic Press. https://doi.org/10.1016/B978-0-12-387691-1.00001-6

15. Roediger, H. L., & Karpicke, J. D. (2006). Test-enhanced learning: Taking memory tests improves long-term retention. *Psychological Science*, 17(3), 249–255. https://doi.org/10.1111/j.1467-9280.2006.01693.x

16. Blasiman, R. N., Dunlosky, J., & Rawson, K. A. (2017). The what, how much, and when of study strategies: Comparing intended versus actual study behaviour. *Memory*, 25(6), 784–792. https://doi.org/10.1080/09658211.2016.1221974

17. Rawson, K. A., & Kintsch, W. (2005). Rereading effects depend on time of test. *Journal of Educational Psychology*, 97(1), 70–80. https://doi.org/10.1037/0022-0663.97.1.70

18. Weinstein, Y., & Sumeracki, M. A. (2019). *Understanding how we learn: A visual guide* (O. Caviglioli, Illus.). Routledge. https://doi.org/10.4324/9780203710463

19. Cepeda, N. J., Vul, E., Rohrer, D., Wixted, J. T., & Pashler, H. (2008). Spacing effects in learning: A temporal ridgeline of optimal retention. *Psychological Science*, 19(11), 1095–1102. https://doi.org/10.1111/j.1467-9280.2008.02209.x

20. Carpenter, S. K., Cepeda, N. J., Rohrer, D., Kang, S. H. K., & Pashler, H. (2012). Using spacing to enhance diverse forms of learning: Review of recent research on implications for instruction. *Educational Psychology Review*, 24, 369–378. https://doi.org/10.1007/s10648-012-9205-z

21. Rasch, B., & Born, J. (2013). About sleep's role in memory. *Physiological Review*, 93(2), 681–766. https://doi.org/10.1152/physrev.00032.2012

22. Deans for Impact. (2015). *The science of learning*. https://www.deansforimpact.org/tools-and-resources/the-science-of-learning

23. Rhodes, M. G., & Castel, A. D. (2008). Memory predictions are influenced by perceptual information: Evidence for metacognitive illusions. *Journal of Experimental Psychology: General*, 137(4), 615–625. https://doi.org/10.1037/a0013684

24. Koriat, A., Bjork, R. A., Sheffer, L., & Bar, S. K. (2004). Predicting one's own forgetting: The role of experience-based and theory-based processes. *Journal of Experimental Psychology: General*, 133(4), 643–656. https://doi.org/10.1037/0096-3445.133.4.643

25. Zimmerman, B. J., & Moylan, A. R. (2009). Self-regulation: Where metacognition and motivation intersect. In D. J. Hacker, J. Dunlosky, & A. C. Graesser (Eds.), *Handbook of metacognition in education* (pp. 299–315). Routledge.

26. Kaminske, A. N., Kuepper-Tetzel, C. E., Nebel, C. L., Sumeracki, M. A., & Ryan, S. P. (2020). Transfer: A review for biology and the life sciences. *CBE—Life Sciences Education*, 19(3), 1–11. https://doi.org/10.1187/cbe.19-11-0227

CHAPTER 7

1. Chase, W., & Simon, H. A. (1973). Perception in chess. *Cognitive Psychology*, 4, 55–81.

2. Hatano, G., & Osawa, K. (1983). Digit memory of grand experts in abacus-derived mental calculation. *Cognition*, 15(1–3), 95–110. https://doi.org/10.1016/0010-0277(83)90035-5

3. Ericsson, K. A., & Kintsch, W. (1995). Long-term working memory. *Psychological Review*, 102(2), 211–245. https://doi.org/10.1037/0033-295X.102.2.211

4. Bédard, J., & Chi, M. T. (1992). Expertise. *Current Directions in Psychological Science*, 1(4), 135–139. https://doi.org/10.1111/1467-8721.ep10769799

5. Feltovich, P. J., Johnson, P. E., Moller, J. H., & Swanson, D. B. (1984). LCS: The role and development of medical knowledge in diagnostic expertise. In W. J. Clancey & E. H. Shortliffe (Eds.), *Readings in medical artificial intelligence* (pp. 275–319). Addison-Wesley.

6. Heller, R., Saltzein, H. D., & Caspe, W. (1992). Heuristics in medical and non-medical decision making. *The Quarterly Journal of Experimental Psychology*, 44(2), 211–235. https://doi.org/10.1080/02724989243000019

7. Ericsson, K. A. (2017). Expertise and individual differences: The search for the structure and acquisition of experts' superior performance. *WIREs Cognitive Science*, 8, e1382. https://doi.org/10.1002/wcs.1382

8. Gladwell, M. (2008). *Outliers: The story of success*. Little, Brown and Company.

9. Ericsson, K. A., Krampe, R. T., & Tesch-Romer, C. (1993). The role of deliberate practice in the acquisition of expert performance. *Psychological Review*, 100(3), 361–406. https://doi.org/10.1098/rsos.190327

10. Ericsson, K. A. (2009). Enhancing the development of professional performance: Implications from the study of deliberate practice. In K. A. Ericsson (Ed.), *Development of professional expertise: Toward measurement of expert performance and design of optimal learning environments* (pp. 405–431). Cambridge University Press. https://doi.org/10.1017/CBO9780511609817.022

11. Ericsson, K. A., & Charness, N. (1994). Expert performance: Its structure and acquisition. *American Psychologist*, 49(8), 725–747. https://doi.org/10.1037/0003-066X.49.8.725

12. Gallagher, A. G., Ritter, M., Champion, H., Higgins, G., Fried, M., Moses, G., Smith, C. D., & Satava, M. (2005). Virtual reality simulation for the operating room: Proficiency-based training as a paradigm shift in surgical skills training. *Annals of Surgery*, 241(2), 364–372. https://doi.org/10.1097/01.sla.0000151982.85062.80

13. Chi, M. T., Feltovich, P. J., & Glaser, R. (1981). Categorization and representation of physics problems by experts and novices. *Cognitive Science*, 5, 121–152. https://doi.org/10.1207/s15516709cog0502_2

14. Witherby, A. E., & Carpenter, S. K. (2021). The rich-get-richer effect: Prior knowledge predicts new learning of domain-relevant information. *Journal of Experimental Psychology: Learning, Memory, and Cognition*, 48(4), 483–498. https://doi.org/10.1037/xlm0000996

15. Wiley, J. (1998). Expertise as mental set: The effects of domain knowledge in creative problem solving. *Memory & Cognition, 26*(4), 716–730. https://doi.org/10.3758/BF03211392

16. Voss, J. F., Vensonder, G., & Spilich, H. (1980). Text generation and recall by high-knowledge and low-knowledge individuals. *Journal of Verbal Learning & Verbal Behavior, 19,* 651–667. https://doi.org/10.1016/S0022-5371(80)90343-6

17. Patel, V. L., & Groen, G. J. (1991). The general and specific nature of medical expertise. In K. A. Ericsson & J. Smith (Eds.), *Toward a general theory of expertise* (pp. 93–125). Cambridge University Press.

18. Schmidt, H. G., & Boshuizen, H. P. A. (1993). On the origin of intermediate effects in clinical case recall. *Memory & Cognition, 21,* 338–351. https://doi.org/10.3758/BF03208266

19. Marchant, G., Robinson, J., Anderson, U., & Schadenwald, M. (1991). Analogical transfer and expertise in legal reasoning. *Organizational Behavior & Human Decision Processes, 48,* 272–290. https://doi.org/10.1016/0749-5978(91)90015-L

20. Frensch, P. A., & Sternberg, R. J. (1989). Expertise and intelligent thinking: When is it worse to know better? In R. J. Sternberg (Ed.), *Advances in the psychology of human intelligence* (Vol. 5, pp. 157–188). Erlbaum.

21. Nickerson, R. S. (1999). How we know—and sometimes misjudge—what others know: Imputing one's own knowledge to others. *Psychological Bulletin, 125,* 737–759. https://doi.org/10.1037/0033-2909.125.6.737

22. Falck, S. (2021). *The psychology of intelligence.* Routledge.

CHAPTER 8

1. Koenig, S. (Host and Executive Producer). (2014–2022). *Serial: Season one* [Audio podcast]. WBEZ Chicago. https://serialpodcast.org/

2. Blair, E. (2022, September 21). *How the investigation of Adnan Syed became a podcast phenomenon.* NPR. https://www.npr.org/2022/09/20/1124141699/serial-adnan-syed

3. Thompson-Cannino, J., Cotton, R., & Torneo, E. (2009). *Picking cotton: Our memoir of injustice and redemption.* St. Martin's Press.

4. Wells, G. L., & Smalarz, L. (2022). Lives destroyed by distorted recollections of fluency, attention, view, and confidence: A sin of bias in eyewitness identification. *Journal of Applied Research in Memory and Cognition, 11*(4), 461–464. https://doi.org/10.1037/mac0000087

5. DeSoto, K. A., & Roediger, H. L. (2014). Positive and negative correlations between confidence and accuracy for the same events in recognition of categorized lists. *Psychological Science*, 25(3), 781–788. https://doi.org/10.1177/0956797613516149

6. Wells, G. L., & Bradfield, A. L. (1998). "Good, you identified the suspect": Feedback to eyewitnesses distorts their reports of the witnessing experience. *Journal of Applied Psychology*, 83(3), 360–376. https://doi.org/10.1037/0021-9010.83.3.360

7. Wells, G. L., & Murray, D. M. (1983). What can psychology say about the Neil v. Biggers criteria for judging eyewitness accuracy? *Journal of Applied Psychology*, 68(3), 347–362. https://doi.org/10.1037//0021-9010.68.3.347

8. Oldmeadow, J., & Fiske, S. T. (2007). System-justifying ideologies moderate status = competence stereotypes: Roles for belief in a just world and social dominance orientation. *European Journal of Social Psychology*, 37, 1135–1148. https://doi.org/10.1002/ejsp.428

9. Bjornstrom, E. E. S., Kaufman, R. L., Peterson, R. D., & Slater, M. D. (2010). Race and ethnic representations of lawreakers and victims in crime news: A national study of television coverage. *Social Problems*, 57(2), 269–293. https://doi.org/10.1525/sp.2010.57.2.269

10. Dottolo, A. L., & Stewart, A. J. (2008). "Don't ever forget now, you're a black man in America": Intersections of race, class and gender in encouters with the police. *Sex Roles*, 59, 350–364. https://doi.org/10.1007/s11199-007-9387-x

11. Loftus, E. F., & Palmer, J. C. (1974). Reconstruction of automobile destruction: An example of the interaction between language and memory. *Journal of Verbal Learning and Verbal Behavior*, 13(5), 585–589. https://doi.org/10.1016/S0022-5371(74)80011-3

12. Loftus, E. F., Miller, D. G., & Burns, H. J. (1978). Semantic integration of verbal information into a visual memory. *Journal of Experimental Psychology: Human Learning and Memory*, 4(1), 19–31. https://doi.org/10.1037/0278-7393.4.1.19

13. Loftus, E. F., & Pickrell, J. E. (1995). The formation of false memories. *Psychiatric Annals*, 25(12), 720–725. https://doi.org/10.3928/0048-5713-19951201-07

14. Morgan, C. A., Southwick, S., Steffian, G., Hazlett, G. A., & Loftus, E. F. (2013). Misinformation can influence memory for recently experienced, highly stressful events. *International Journal of Law and Psychiatry*, 36(1), 11–17. https://doi.org/10.1016/j.ijlp.2012.11.002

15. Kocab, K., & Sporer, S. L. (2016). The weapon focus effect for person identification and descriptions: A meta-analysis. In M. K. Miller & B. H. Bornstein (Eds.), *Advances in psychology and law* (pp. 71–117). Springer International Publishing. https://doi.org/10.1007/978-3-319-29406-3_3

16. Lynn, S. J., Kirsch, I., Terhune, D. B., & Green, J. P. (2020). Myths and misconceptions about hypnosis and suggestion: Separating fact and fiction. *Applied Cognitive Psychology*, 34, 1253–1264. https://doi.org/10.1002/acp.3730

17. Wells, G. L., Kovera, M. B., Douglass, A. B., Brewer, N., Meissner, C. A., & Wixted, J. T. (2020). Policy and procedure recommendations for the collection and preservation of eyewitness identification evidence. *Law and Human Behavior*, 44(1), 3–36. https://doi.org/10.1037/lhb0000359

18. La Rooy, D., Brubacher, S. P., Aromäki-Stratos, A., Cyr, M., Hershkowitz, I., Korkman, J., Myklebust, T., Naka, M., Peixoto, C. E., Roberts, K. P., Stewart, H., & Lamb, M. E. (2015). The NICHD protocol: A review of an internationally-used evidence-based tool for training child forensic interviewers. *Journal of Criminological Research, Policy and Practice*, 1(2), 76–89. https://doi.org/10.1108/JCRPP-01-2015-0001

19. Megreya, A. M., & Burton, A. M. (2008). Matching faces to photographs: Poor performance in eyewitness memory (without the memory). *Journal of Experimental Psychology: Applied*, 14(4), 364–372. https://doi.org/10.1037/a0013464

20. Kramer, R. S., Mohamed, S., & Hardy, S. C. (2019). Unfamiliar face matching with driving license and passport photographs. *Perception*, 48(2), 175–184. https://doi.org/10.1177/0301006619826495

21. Sporer, S. L. (2001). The cross-race effect: Beyond recognition of faces in the laboratory. *Psychology, Public Policy, and Law*, 7(1), 170–200. https://doi.org/10.1037//1076-8971.7.1.170

22. Wells, G. L. (1993). What do we know about eyewitness identification? *American Psychologist*, 48(5), 553–571. https://doi.org/10.1037/0003-066X.48.5.553

23. Hopper, J. (2018, September 27). How reliable are the memories of sexual assault victims? *Scientific American*. https://blogs.scientificamerican.com/observations/how-reliable-are-the-memories-of-sexual-assault-victims/

Printed in the United States
by Baker & Taylor Publisher Services